Blogging: The Ultimate Guide

Blogging:
The Ultimate Guide

Barry Miller

Larsen & Keller
www.larsen-keller.com

Blogging: The Ultimate Guide
Barry Miller
ISBN: 979-8-88836-098-9 (Hardback)

Larsen & Keller

Published by Larsen and Keller Education,
5 Penn Plaza,
19th Floor,
New York, NY 10001, USA

Cataloging-in-Publication Data

Blogging : the ultimate guide / Barry Miller.
      p. cm.
Includes bibliographical references and index.
ISBN 979-8-88836-098-9
1. Blogs--Handbooks, manuals, etc. 2. Blogs--Vocational guidance. I. Miller, Barry.
PN4567.2 .B56 2023
006.752--dc23

For more information regarding Larsen and Keller Education and its products, please visit the publisher's website www.larsen-keller.com

Table of Contents

Preface

A blog is an informational website or a discussion published on the World Wide Web that consists of informal diary-style posts by a single or multiple authors. Multi-author blogs from media outlets, newspapers, think tanks and advocacy groups contribute significantly to blog traffic. Some blogs can provide a commentary on a particular subject such as politics, sports, etc., while others can function as personal diaries or act to advertise a company or brand. Companies use blogs to enhance the organizational culture, communication and employee engagement. They also use them as a tool of marketing, public relations and branding. Most blogs are text-based but they can also feature photographs, art, videos, music and audio. They can be classified into personal blogs, group blogs, political blogs, travel blogs, vlogs, reverse blogs, etc. This textbook unfolds the innovative aspects of blogging, which will be crucial for the holistic understanding of this Internet tool. It also explores all the important genres of blogging and their importance in the modern scenario. Those with an interest to start a blog or make a successful career in blogging will find this book full of crucial and unexplored ideas.

A detailed account of the significant topics covered in this book is provided below:

Chapter 1- The World Wide Web is populated by diverse informational websites and discussions that consists of discrete, informal diary-style posts. These are known as blogs. They generally provide information on a specific topic or subject. They are a combination of content - art, videos, photographs, music and audio. This chapter introduces in brief about the modern aspects of blogs and blogging, and includes topics on the ways to start a personal blog or a micro blog and be a professional and successful blogger.

Chapter 2- Blogs can be of different types, as per the content written or delivered. Blogs may focus on a particular subject, such as travel blogs, fashion blogs, photography blogs, art blogs, etc. The diverse kinds of blogs, which are in vogue in the digital world today, have been thoroughly discussed in this chapter. It also provides a detailed explanation on the typical challenges faced by an amateur blogger and their solutions and includes ways to run a blog for a creative business, starting a vlog, etc.

Chapter 3- The common platforms used for the creation of blogs include Blogger and WordPress. This chapter provides a detailed understanding of the diverse aspects involved in the creation and use of a Blogger account. It includes an overview of the ways to back up the contents of a blog, delete a blog, set up a Google+ authorship for Blogger, schedule a post on Blogger, etc.

Chapter 4- WordPress is an open-source and free content management system, which is based on PHP and MySQL. Some of its key features are a plugin architecture and template system. WordPress is perhaps the most popular website management globally. The chapter closely examines the key aspects of blogging in WordPress, such as creating a WordPress blog, creating a page on WordPress blog, adding a new post in WordPress and adding or deleting a WordPress post, etc. to provide an extensive understanding of this blogging platform.

Chapter 5- Blogs can attract an audience if it is unique, attractive and completely functional. The design of a blog is the next crucial thing after the quality of content. This chapter has been carefully written to provide an insight into the designing of a blog and includes a wide content, from choosing a blog name, to making a blog layout, changing the font on Blogger to adding social networking options to the blog.

I would like to make a special mention of my publisher who considered me worthy of this opportunity and also supported me throughout the process. I would also like to thank the editing team at the back-end who extended their help whenever required.

Barry Miller

Understanding Blogs and Blogging

The World Wide Web is populated by diverse informational websites and discussions that consists of discrete, informal diary-style posts. These are known as blogs. They generally provide information on a specific topic or subject. They are a combination of content - art, videos, photographs, music and audio. This chapter introduces in brief about the modern aspects of blogs and blogging, and includes topics on the ways to start a personal blog or a micro blog and be a professional and successful blogger.

Blog

A blog (shortening of "weblog") is an online journal or informational website displaying information in the reverse chronological order, with latest posts appearing first. It is a platform where a writer or even a group of writers share their views on an individual subject.

Blogs are typically run by an individual or a small group of people to present information in a conversational style. However now there are tons of corporate blogs that produce tons of informational and thought-leadership style content.

What is Difference Between Blog and Website

Blogs are a type of website. The only real difference between a blog and other types of website is that blogs are regularly updated with new content displayed in a reversed chronological order (newer posts first).

Typical websites are static in nature where content is organized in pages, and they are not updated frequently. Whereas a blog is dynamic, and it is usually updated more frequently. Some bloggers publish multiple new articles a day.

Blogs can be a part of the larger website. Often businesses have a blog section where they regularly create content to inform and educate their customers. Because you can use WordPress to create a website and blog, a lot of business owners use WordPress to build their small business website.

In simple terms, all blogs can be a website or part of a website. However, not all websites can be called blogs.

Types

There are many different types of blogs, differing not only in the type of content, but also in the way that content is delivered or written.

- Personal blogs

  The personal blog is an ongoing online diary or commentary written by an individual, rather than a corporation or organization. While the vast majority of personal blogs attract very few readers, other than the blogger's immediate family and friends, a small number of personal blogs have become popular, to the point that they have attracted lucrative advertising sponsorship. A tiny number of personal bloggers have become famous, both in the online community and in the real world.

- Collaborative blogs or group blogs

  A type of weblog in which posts are written and published by more than one author. The majority of high-profile collaborative blogs are based around a single uniting theme, such as politics, technology or advocacy. In recent years, the blogosphere has seen the emergence and growing popularity of more collaborative efforts, often set up by already established bloggers wishing to pool time and resources, both to reduce the pressure of maintaining a popular website and to attract a larger readership.

- Microblogging

  Microblogging is the practice of posting small pieces of digital content—which could be text, pictures, links, short videos, or other media—on the Internet. Microblogging offers a portable communication mode that feels organic and spontaneous to many users. It has captured the public imagination, in part because the short posts are easy to read on the go or when waiting. Friends use it to keep in touch, business associates use it to coordinate meetings or share useful resources, and celebrities and politicians (or their publicists) microblog about concert dates, lectures, book releases, or tour schedules. A wide and growing range of add-on tools enables sophisticated updates and interaction with other applications. The resulting profusion of functionality is helping to define new possibilities for this type of communication. Examples of these include Twitter, Facebook, Tumblr and, by far the largest, WeiBo.

- Corporate and organizational blogs

A blog can be private, as in most cases, or it can be for business or not-for-profit organization or government purposes. Blogs used internally, and only available to employees via an Intranet are called corporate blogs. Companies use internal corporate blogs enhance the communication, culture and employee engagement in a corporation. Internal corporate blogs can be used to communicate news about company policies or procedures, build employee esprit de corps and improve morale. Companies and other organizations also use external, publicly accessible blogs for marketing, branding, or public relations purposes. Some organizations have a blog authored by their executive; in practice, many of these executive blog posts are penned by a ghostwriter, who makes posts in the style of the credited author. Similar blogs for clubs and societies are called club blogs, group blogs, or by similar names; typical use is to inform members and other interested parties of club and member activities.

- Aggregated blogs

Individuals or organization may aggregate selected feeds on specific topic, product or service and provide combined view for its readers. This allows readers to concentrate on reading instead of searching for quality on-topic content and managing subscriptions. Many such aggregation called planets from name of Planet (software) that perform such aggregation, hosting sites usually have *planet*.

- By genre

Some blogs focus on a particular subject, such as political blogs, journalism blogs, health blogs, travel blogs (also known as *travelogs*), gardening blogs, house blogs, book blogs, fashion blogs, beauty blogs, lifestyle blogs, party blogs, wedding blogs, photography blogs, project blogs, psychology blogs, sociology blogs, education blogs, niche blogs, classical music blogs, quizzing blogs, legal blogs (often referred to as a blawgs), or dreamlogs. How-to/ Tutorial blogs are becoming increasing popular. Two common types of genre blogs are art blogs and music blogs. A blog featuring discussions especially about home and family is not uncommonly called a mom blog and one made popular is by Erica Diamond who created Womenonthefence.com which is syndicated to over two million readers monthly. While not a legitimate type of blog, one used for the sole purpose of spamming is known as a splog.

- By media type

A blog comprising videos is called a vlog, one comprising links is called a linklog, a site containing a portfolio of sketches is called a sketchblog or one comprising photos is called a photoblog. Blogs with shorter posts and mixed media types are called tumblelogs. Blogs that are written on typewriters and then scanned are called typecast or typecast blogs. A rare type of blog hosted on the Gopher Protocol is known as a phlog.

- By device

A blog can also be defined by which type of device is used to compose it. A blog written by a mobile device like a mobile phone or PDA could be called a moblog. One early blog was Wearable Wireless Webcam, an online shared diary of a person's personal life combining text, video, and pictures transmitted live from a wearable computer and EyeTap device to a web site. This practice of semi-automated blogging with live video together with text was referred to as sousveillance. Such journals have been used as evidence in legal matters.

- Reverse blog

A reverse blog is composed by its users rather than a single blogger. This system has the characteristics of a blog, and the writing of several authors. These can be written by several contributing authors on a topic, or opened up for anyone to write. There is typically some limit to the number of entries to keep it from operating like a web forum.

Community and Cataloging

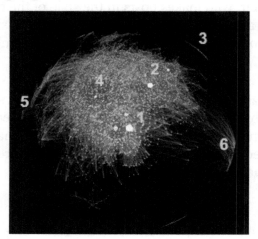

- Blogosphere

The collective community of all blogs and blog authors, particularly notable and widely read blogs, is known as the *blogosphere*. Since all blogs are on the internet by definition, they may be seen as interconnected and socially networked, through blogrolls, comments, linkbacks (refbacks, trackbacks or pingbacks), and backlinks. Discussions "in the blogosphere" are occasionally used by the media as a gauge of public opinion on various issues. Because new, untapped communities of bloggers and their readers can emerge in the space of a few years, Internet marketers pay close attention to "trends in the blogosphere".

- Blog search engines

Several blog search engines have been used to search blog contents, such as Bloglines, BlogScope, and Technorati. Technorati was one of the more popular blog search engines, but the website stopped indexing blogs and assigning authority scores in May 2014. The research community is working on going beyond simple keyword search, by inventing new ways to navigate through huge amounts of information present in the blogosphere, as demonstrated by projects like BlogScope, which was shut down in 2012.

- Blogging communities and directories

  Several online communities exist that connect people to blogs and bloggers to other bloggers. Some of these communities include Indiblogger, Blogadda, Blog Chatter, BlogCatalog and MyBlogLog. Interest-specific blogging platforms are also available. For instance, Blogster has a sizable community of political bloggers among its members. Global Voices aggregates international bloggers, "with emphasis on voices that are not ordinarily heard in international mainstream media."

- Blogging and advertising

  It is common for blogs to feature banner advertisements or promotional content, either to financially benefit the blogger, support website hosting costs, or to promote the blogger's favorite causes or products. The popularity of blogs has also given rise to "fake blogs" in which a company will create a fictional blog as a marketing tool to promote a product.

As the popularity of blogging continues to rise, the commercialisation of blogging is rapidly increasing. Many corporations and companies collaborate with bloggers to increase advertising and engage online communities towards their products. In the book *Fans, Bloggers, and Gamers*, Henry Jenkins stated that "Bloggers take knowledge in their own hands, enabling successful navigation within and between these emerging knowledge cultures. One can see such behaviour as co-optation into commodity culture insofar as it sometimes collaborates with corporate interests, but one can also see it as increasing the diversity of media culture, providing opportunities for greater inclusiveness, and making more responsive to consumers."

How to Start a Blog

Part 1. Creating a Successful Blog

1. Come up with a list of interests: Before you define your blog's intention, you should have a general idea of what you want to write about. The sky is the limit when it comes to your blog's category, but common topics include the following:

- Gaming

- Style

- Politics/Social Justice/Activism

- Cooking/Food

- Travel

- Business/Company

2. Know what not to blog about: Things like private information—both yours and other people's—and personal details that you don't want to share with people close to you shouldn't be topics for your blog.

- If you have a job that required you to sign an NDA (non-disclosure agreement), you should avoid discussing activities or topics outlined in the NDA.

- Blogging about other people is fine as long as you don't harass or discriminate against them, but be aware that they may see your content and retaliate.

3. Consider your blog's intention: While having in mind a blog topic is a good start, your blog needs specific direction in order to get off the ground. Common reasons for blogging include one (or a combination) of the following, though you can certainly find your own inspiration:

- Teach something — Best-suited to instructional blogs (e.g., DIY projects).

- Document your experience — Good for travel blogs, fitness challenges, and so on.

- Entertain — Well-suited to a variety of mediums such as comedy writing, fan-fiction, and so on.

- Call to action — Commonly used for your business or company blog.

- Inspire others — This is a category that can stand on its own, but may best fit any of the other intentions in this topic.

4. Check out other blogs in your category: Once you've established your blog's topic and goal, research other blogs that use the same topic and your preferred style of writing to see how they engage their audiences.

- You shouldn't outright copy a blog you admire, but you can take inspiration from the tone, layout, or language used for the blog content itself.

5. Brainstorm blog specifics: The last two things you should know before you actually make your

blog are the blog's name and how you want the blog to look:

- Blog name — Come up with a name that you feel comfortable sharing with others. This may be a combination of your interests, your blog's content, and a nickname; just make sure that your blog's title is both unique and easy to remember.

- Blog design — You probably won't be able to design your blog's layout exactly the way you want to, but having a general idea of the color scheme and font type before you go to create your blog will make it easier to find a template you like.

6. Create your blog using a reputable platform: Common blog platforms include WordPress, Blogger, and Tumblr, but you can choose any commonly used service you like. Once you've selected a service, your blog creation process will usually look something like this:

- Open the service's website on your computer.

- Create an account (preferably a free one to start).

- Enter your desired blog name, then pick a URL.

- Select a blog layout and any other requested details.

7. Promote your blog on social media: Once you've created your blog and made a few posts, you can increase your blog traffic by posting a link to your blog on social media sites such as Facebook and Twitter.

- You might even consider using the blog's address in your bio or as your "Company Website" on social media.

8. Research keywords for your posts: "Keywords" are words which both pertain to your blog's topic and have a high search engine rating. Using keywords in your blog posts will make it easier for people who look up those words to find your content.

- Keyword generator sites such as http://ubersuggest.io/ or https://keywordtool.io/ will come up with a list of words that relate to your blog's topic.

- Re-check the keywords you use every time you create a blog post.

- If you fit the keywords into your posts in a natural way, search engines will be more likely to pick up on your blog than if you just scatter them throughout the posts.

9. Get your blog indexed by Google: Ensuring that your blog is indexed by Google will increase

your search engine ranking, making it easier for people to find your blog when they look up related keywords.

10. Use images in your posts: One thing that search engines tend to prioritize over all else is image use, so make sure your posts have high-quality images attached to them.

- You may get bonus points for original photos.

- Users tend to appreciate visual input alongside text, so adding images to your blog is a good idea even if you aren't worried about search engine optimization.

11. Keep posting content: Little will cause your blog to stop drawing in traffic faster than not posting for a long period of time (or posting erratically). Develop a posting schedule that allows you to post at least once per week and stick to it.

- Missing a post by a day or two once in a while is fine, though you should consider making on social media a note that your post will be late.

- Fresh content will also help keep your blog near the top of search engine results.

Part 2. Creating a Blog in WordPress

1. Open WordPress. Go to https://wordpress.com/ in your computer's web browser.

2. Click Get Started. It's a link in the upper-right corner of the page.

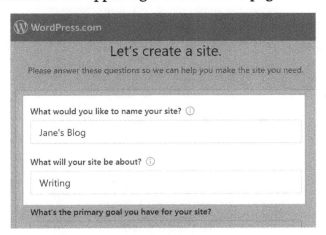

3. Fill out the blog creation form. Enter your information into the following fields:

- What would you like to name your site? — Enter your blog's name here.

- What will your site be about? — Type in a one-word category, then click a category that fits your blog in the resulting drop-down menu.

- What's the primary goal you have for your site? — Type in a one-word category, then click a category that fits your blog in the resulting drop-down menu.

- How comfortable are you with creating a website? — Click one of the numbers at the bottom of the page.

4. Click Continue. It's at the very bottom of the page.

5. Enter your preferred address for your blog. In the top text box, type in whatever you want your blog's URL name to be.

- Don't include the "www" or ".com" part of the URL here.

6. Click Select next to the "Free" option: This option will appear below the text box. Doing so selected the free address for your blog.

7. Click Start with Free: It's on the left side of the page. Doing so will take you to the account creation page.

8. Enter an email address: Type the email address you want to use to create your account into the "Your email address" text box.

9. Enter a password: Type a password for your account into the "Choose a password" text box.

10. Click Continue: It's a blue button at the bottom of the page.

11. Confirm your email address: While you're waiting for WordPress to finalize your account details, do the following:

- Open your WordPress email inbox in a new tab.

- Click the "Activate (blog name)" email from "WordPress".

- Click Click here to Confirm Now in the email body.

- Close the tab once it finishes loading.

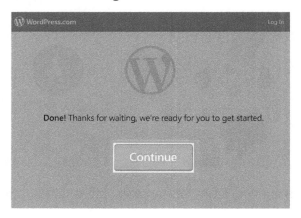

12. Click Continue: It's in the middle of the original tab on which you created your WordPress account.

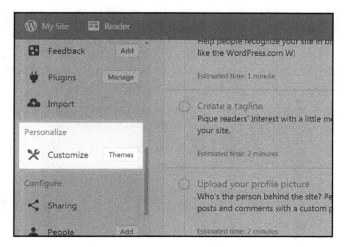

13. Add a theme to your blog: The "theme" dictates how your blog looks. Scroll down to the "Customize" heading, click Themes, and select the theme you want to use for your blog. You can then click Activate this design at the top of the page.

- You might want to click Free in the upper-right side of the page to see results for free themes only.

14. Start writing: You can start your first blog post by clicking Write in the upper-right side of the window to bring up the post window; at this point, you're free to begin creating content for your blog.

How to Start a Blog for Free

There are millions of blogs online that allow people to share their personal and professional opinions. Free blogging is available on user-friendly sites that work by updating a pre-designed template. Learn how to start a blog for free.

Part 1. Research Free Blog Services

1. Visit free blogging sites to see examples of blogging templates and features: The following are the most popular sites for free blogging:

- WordPress: The most popular free blogging platform, WordPress provides you plenty of templates and customizable features. If you want a more in depth control of your features and built in analytics, this is the best platform for a free blog.

- Blogger: Google bought this popular blogging platform, and it is considered the most user-friendly option. It may not have as many customizable features as WordPress, but it is preferable for someone with fewer computer skills. Create a Google account, and click on the "More" tab to find the sign up on Google.com.

- Tumblr: This is free blogging designed for visual artists and photographers. If you are excited about posting photos and videos, they can be combined seamlessly into the available templates.

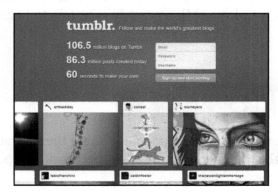

2. Decide if you want to own your own domain name.

- Free blogging sites host a domain that leads with their website and includes your name on the URL. Services like WordPress and Blogger allow you to buy your domain name for $10 to $17 per year. Although this is not technically free, it is a good idea if you are blogging for professional reasons.

Part 2. Start your Free Blog

1. Go to wordpress.com, blogger.com or tumblr.com: Click on the option to start to sign up for a new account.

- On Blogger, you will need to confirm your Google profile before signing up for your blog.

2. Create your online profile: You will need to add information about your email, name and a password. Make sure it is something secure that you can remember.

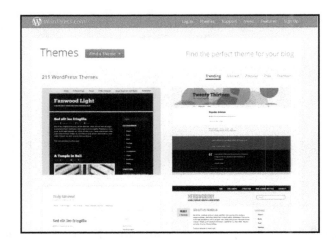

3. Choose your template: Preview several options. There are hundreds to choose from on these 3 sites.

4. Verify your account: Before your blog is available to the public, you will need to access your email and click on the verification link.

Part 3. Learn to Post Effectively

1. Start writing: Many people simply blog about what is relevant in their lives.

- When in doubt, keep it short. People usually like to scan for topics that are important to them.

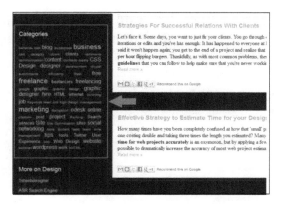

2. Use word tags and clouds to help people sift through your posts: Instead of listing blog posts by date, use the free options to categorize them by topic. Each post will apply to several topics.

- Each blogging platform gives you the opportunity to associate different keywords with your post. These will help you categorize them for your blog and on search engines.

3. Post pictures: Include a relevant picture in each post. Each platform allows you to change the position of the photo and its size, as well as keep a media library.

- Keep a camera phone or camera with you at all times, so that you can get unique images for your posts.

- Some people sort through Google images to find media that goes with their post. Beware of using copy written images in your blog.

4. Link your blog to your social media accounts: Add widgets to your blog that bring up Facebook, Twitter or LinkedIn posts. This is especially important if you are trying to increase the number of followers or friends you have.

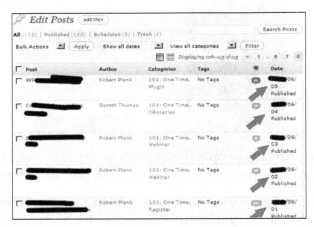

5. Post at least once per week: You must remain consistent to encourage people to read your blog.

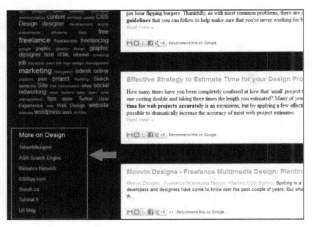

6. Post links to other blogs or interesting topics: Your blog should regularly cross-reference other interesting people so that it becomes a source for reliable and fun information.

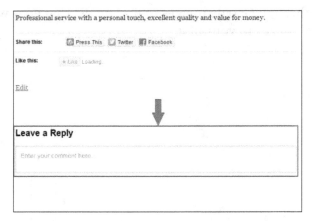

7. Allow readers to comment: Create a conversation with each post.

8. Provide your expertise: If you are writing a professional or hobby blog, giving your opinions on the industry will get more people to subscribe and read daily.

Part 4. Promote your Free Blog

1. Post about hot topics: Things that are in the news will bring more readers to your blog.

2. Take writing classes, if you feel your writing is sub par.

- The most popular blogs involve people who can articulate a thought or argument. Make your main point early on in the article. Support it with evidence, such as links to news articles or photos.

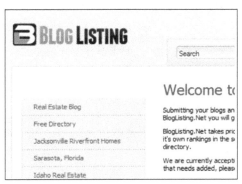

3. Start submitting to directories: Many sites keep a comprehensive list of bloggers.

- Blog directories can drive some traffic your way. Consider submitting to blog listing, blog-arama and globe of blogs. Search for other options using your search engine.

4. Go to Technorati.com to claim your blog: This site functions as a directory and ranking system for bloggers.

- Create an account. Then, write a description of your blog and the URL. You should see increased traffic if you post regularly.

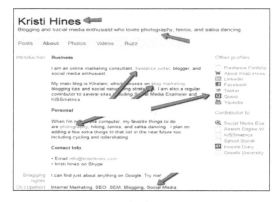

5. Learn search engine optimization (SEO): SEO allows you to use Google and other search engine crawler rules to your benefit. You will be ranked higher on search engines if you follow their best practices.

6. Become part of the blogging community: Regularly read other people's blogs and comment on them. Post your blog's name in addition to your name.

- Important SEO topics include using keywords in the article, using keywords in the headline, learning to write meta tags, naming your images correctly and simplifying URLs.

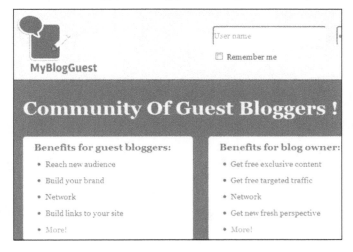

7. Serve as a guest blogger: Trade blogger spots with a writer you like. You can share subscribers.

How to Create a Personal Blog

Blogging has become one of the more popular pastimes on the internet. Some people blog for money, others blog about current events, and others blog for humor. The list goes on. Increasingly, bloggers are use weblogs as a personal journal, preferring to keep it out of the spotlight. If you're someone who wants to start a personal blog, it's really quite easy.

Method 1. Choosing your Blog

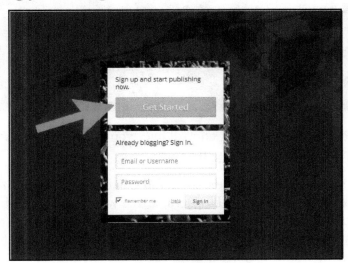

1. Select a blog host: A host is a website whose blogging platform you'll use in order to start blogging. With the rise of the internet, dozens of blogging hosts have risen to prominence, many of them easy to use for people who know next to nothing about computers. There are plenty of free hosts in addition to hosts for which you need to pay. Here are a list of just a few:

- Free blog hosts
    - Wordpress.com
    - Blogger
    - Tumblr
    - SimpleSite
    - Wix.com
- Blog hosts with fees
    - GoDaddy
    - Bluehost
    - HostGator
    - Hostmonster

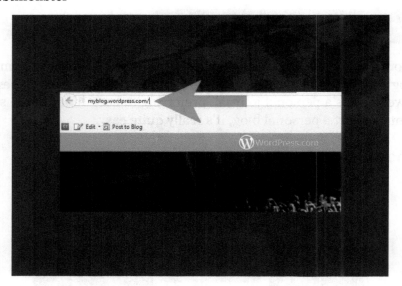

2. Determine how much control you want control over your URL: If you use a free blogging platform, your URL is going to look something like this:

If you intend for your blog to be strictly personal, and you don't anticipate the need to build your own brand or start reaching out to other bloggers, a free web hosting service will do you fine. If, however, you believe that you may want to show your blog to other people and build your online presence at some point in the future, a paid hosting service will allow you to create a blog with a distinct and personalized URL. In that case, your URL can look like this.

- Know the differences between free hosting services and paid hosting services. Mainly, paid hosting services offer much more control over the look of the website design, as well as offering more web tools with which to personalize blogs (plugins, widgets, buttons, etc.). Although the amateur blogger probably won't need a paid hosting service, it's useful to know what you can and can't do with a free platform:

- Generally, free hosting services offer a few basic pre-made templates for bloggers to choose from when designing the look of the website. Paid hosting services generally offer a greater variety of templates to choose from, as well as giving the blogger the option of designing the look of the website from the bottom up.

- The biggest misconception with Wordpress. Wordpress.com and Wordpress.org are different platforms that both provide the same purpose. They are both powered with Wordpress but with Wordpress.com your site will be hosted by the company vs. with Wordpress.org which you are hosting your self.

- Certain plugins are available only to people who pay for hosting services. A plugin is a tool that bloggers use to customize their blog. (A rotating tab, for example, is a cool plugin that allows viewers to see more of your content on tabbed panels.) Countless other plugins exist for paid hosting services.

- *This seems to be the bottom line*: If you're just interested in creating a vehicle for your thoughts, these bells and whistles are probably superfluous. If, however, you take pride in the design of your website and like the idea of creating different tools for potential viewers to someday interact with, having more power to customize your weblog may be a good decision.

- Get familiar with the ins and outs of whatever hosting service you decide to use. How do you italicize a title? How will you create an outbound link to another website? These are questions that you'll ask yourself as you start blogging. Although your familiarity with your blogging platform will increase the more you blog, it's important to explore the different options you have with your blog. You often don't know what is possible until you try it.

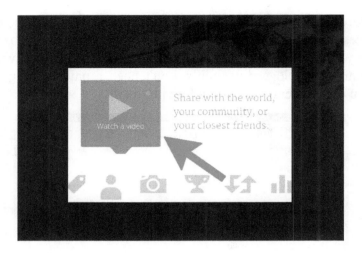

Some blogs offer an interactive video or slideshow to new users. If such a video or slideshow exists on your new blogging platform, be sure to watch it. These tutorials are packed with useful tips and hints, and will get you blogging faster and better.

Method 2. Getting Started

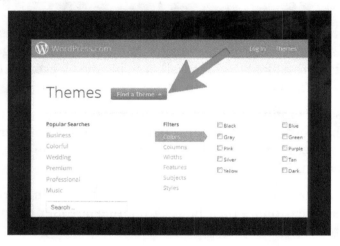

1. Design the look of your blog: Every time you log in to your blog, the design of it ideally should motivate you to write. For some people, a simple write background, mimicking a blank page, sets the heart aflutter. For others, an intricate houndstooth pattern does the trick. How do you want your blog to look.

- Choose a simple background over a loud and in-your-face one, although do what pleases you most. Here are some ideas for simple backgrounds you can mull over:

  ◦ A photograph of you and your family on vacation

  ◦ A simple, unobtrusive pattern that provides texture but doesn't take away from the words

  ◦ A map of picture of a map

- ° A writing object, such as a fountain pen, typewriter, or ream of paper

- ° A simple background in your favorite color

2. Look for a "keep private" check box within the options setting of your blog server: If you want your blog to be personal and de-indexed from search results, so that only you see it, check this option. In many blogs, there is also an option which allows you to keep your blog entirely private, where a password is required to access it. Look for this option if you want your blog to be truly secret.

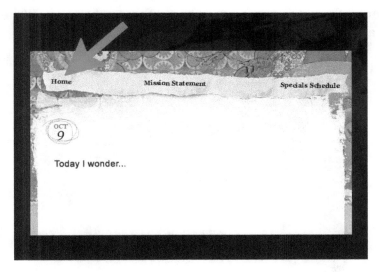

3. Design your blog for simple navigation: If you make categories into which you place your blog posts, try ordering the categories by popularity. Why put the blog post you visit least right up there at the top, and the blog post you visit most near the bottom? Design with simple navigation in mind.

- • Reduce the clutter. Just because you have the option of creating dozens of plugins and widgets doesn't mean you need to use them. If this blog is indeed about you and your thoughts, make *them* stand out instead of extraneous stuff.

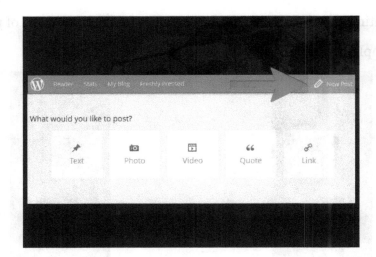

4. Create your first blog post: In many public blogs, your first post is a short explanation of who you are (some secrets are kept) and why you decided to blog. It's an online introduction of sorts. Because you're building a personal blog, however, you need not be so formal in your first post.

- Write about what motivated you to start a blog. It may help to put things into writing. This is often a cathartic act, too, releasing certain tensions and stress. Try it on for size and see how it feels.

- Write about what you intended to write about. Jump right in. Your blog can turn into a diary of sorts, or it can be a place where you gather interesting articles from around the web and comment on them. Of course, it can be anything in between. Write or post about what makes you happy.

Method 3. Maintaining your Blog

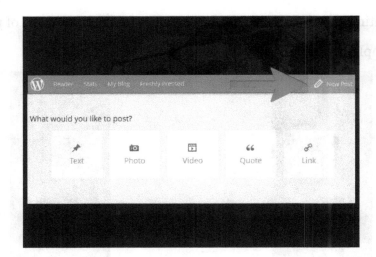

1. Try to blog every day: Even if nothing of note has transpired, it's important to set aside time to blog. Getting in the rhythm of blogging can be difficult, but pretty soon you'll be doing it by instinct: Like the first day of school, it may be a bit awkward at first, but you soon make friends and grow comfortable in your new environment.

- Think about special themed days when posting. If you wanted, for example, you could have "Maniac Mondays," where each Monday, you blog about one person whose crazy ideas changed the world. This lends your blog some structure and helps keep you writing, even when you're not exactly sure what to write about.

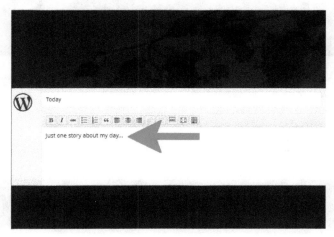

2. Keep posts short: If you're having trouble writing, keep your blog posts short. A blog can be different from a diary, expose, or news article. It's meant to be digested quickly, to offer interlocking pieces of evidence and tie them together concisely. Keep these three guidelines in mind when you start blogging:

- A blog can be a place for reading. Jot things down quickly rather than write extended essays on them. A "Hey, look at this!" seems to be a lot more effective in blog form than a "And these are all the reasons why I'm better than you."

- Use links. Link out to other interesting pieces of content out on the web. For one, it will help you remember interesting sites that you stumble across. Second, it will save you the time to paraphrase what's going on — unless that's what you're trying to do.

- Revisit old themes. Just because you've already written a blog doesn't mean you need to file it away in a musty place. Revisit your feelings about that article in a new article, for example.

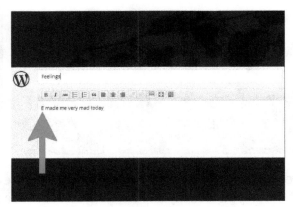

3. Use first letters of names when writing about others to maintain anonymity: For example, "E

made me very mad today; I've had it up to here with his selfishness." This ensures that no feelings will be hurt should someone stumble upon your blog.

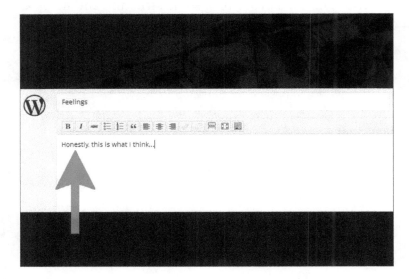

4. Be truthful: Feelings do not always make sense! Fortunately, they don't have to. All that matters is that your emotions end up blogged rather than expressed as an ulcer. Remember that your blog exists only as an outlet for you. You don't have to worry about pleasing other people if you don't want to.

- Often, you'll find that writing about something helps you understand it. So even if you don't quite understand it yet, being truthful about it can help you figure it out. Writing is an act of self-discovery. If you're truthful when you write, you're sure to discover things about yourself that you didn't know about.

5. Learn from your posts: Once you have blogged for a while, go back and review. Have you learned the sources of stress in your life? Can you identify any running themes? Is a particular person toxic to your emotional health.

6. Interact with your community of readers and commentors: Even if you are anonymous, your blog may still be enjoyed by readers and commentors. Often, they leave a comment underneath your article expressing praise, opinions, or questions. Successful bloggers understand that interacting with these fans of your work is an important part of spurring readership.

- Respond to most, not all, comments: Often, a reader will leave a comment urging you to keep on writing. A simple "Thank you, appreciated," might be a good way to respond. Other times, people will ramble off-topic or express very controversial opinions. It is not necessary to respond to each and every one of your commenters if you don't wish to.

- Include a call to action at the end of a post (optional): Obviously, if you don't intend to show your blog to other people, a call to action is unnecessary. But if you enjoy the thought of soliciting the opinion of your readers, include something like "What was your favorite Christmas present?" or "What do you think about the Federal stimulus?" in an appropriately themed post.

7. Share your writing with close friends and family: The people closest to you care about your thoughts and feelings. Although you've probably started a personal blog as a placeholder for your own thoughts and emotions, it can be powerful to share those experiences with other people. What you're doing is starting a conversation, and conversation can be enlightening, uplifting, and powerful.

- For example, maybe you've just been given a diagnosis of cancer and decided to start a blog to document your journey. You only intended for it to be seen by you. But what you grew to understand as you started writing was that sharing your deepest fears and desires actually brought you closer to the people around you; it made you more human. Sharing this realization with your close friends and family can be incredibly freeing.

Blogging

blogging involved a personal web log, in which a person would journal about their day. From "web log" came the term "blog."

Like most new innovations on the Internet, many entrepreneurs saw marketing potential in having a blog, and blogging took off from there. Not only can a blog be used for marketing, but also, a blog can be a home business in and of itself.

Why Blogging is so Popular

There are several reasons why entrepreneurs have turned to blogging:

1. Search engines love new content, and as a result, blogging is a great search engine optimization (SEO) tool.

2. Blogging provides an easy way to keep your customers and clients up-to-date on what's going on, let them know about new deals, and provide tips. The more a customer comes to your blog, the more likely they are to spend money.

3. A blog allows you to build trust and rapport with your prospects. Not only can you show off what you know, building your expertise and credibility, but because people can post comments and interact with you, they can get to know you, and hopefully, will trust you enough to buy from you.

1. Blogs can make money. Along with your product or service, blogs can generate income from other options, such as advertising and affiliate products.

2. Blogging is flexible and portable, making it a great option for people who be a lifestyle entrepreneur.

Is there a Downside to Blogging

Blogging is popular because it works as a marketing tool and makes money. But blogging isn't all rainbows and unicorns in the world of online income. Before starting a blog as a means to make money or to promote your existing business, you should consider these potential downsides:

1. Blogging requires a great deal of time. For blogs to be effective at SEO and engaging readers, it needs to be updated regularly. The Internet is littered with abandoned blogs that

haven't been updated in months or even years. The success of blogging comes from having people return, and they only return when there's new stuff to read. That means generating content at least several times a week, which takes time.

2. You need ideas to write about. To keep the content coming, you have to have ideas to write about. The good news is that you don't have to write it all. You can have guest writers or hire freelancers. Another option is to curate content from others or do an alternative post, such as using video. Finally, you can buy private label right (PLR) content, and modify it for posting on your blog.

3. The payoff isn't immediate. One of the biggest frustrations with blogging is that it's time-consuming with little payoff in the beginning. It takes time to build up a readership and momentum.

How to Learn about Micro Blogging

You have heard about blogging and micro-blogging, but you are unsure of their use. They both have their purposes, advantages and level of involvement. Micro blogging is great for those that are on the go and want to keep in touch with their friends as they move through their day.

Steps

1. Learn the difference:

- Blog - (short for weblog) is a personal online journal that is frequently updated and intended for general public consumption.

- Micro Blog - a form of multimedia blogging that allows users to send brief text updates or micromedia such as photos or audio clips and publish them. Some micro-blogging platform have limits as to the maximum number of characters per post. Twitter for example limits you to 140 characters per tweet. Because of this limitation, many long URLs in posts are shorten using URL shorteners.

    ◦ Both bloggers and micro-bloggers have a variety of third party software or plug-ins for their browsers to simplify the process.

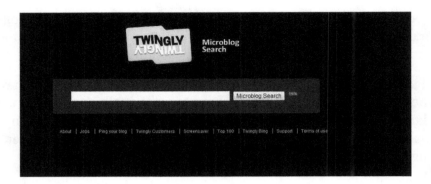

2. Choose a medium or media for micro-blogging: There are a number of clients that will allow you to post quick updates from your smart phone, mobile device, or desktop. These clients also will help you to keep track of activity throughout the day, since a big part of micro-blogging is interaction and re-posting others' content. Texting is one easy way to micro-blog throughout the day if you're not near a computer. You can also keep a desktop client running in the background throughout the day and set up notifications to let you know when someone has mentioned you or re-blogged your content.

3. Get into the habit of micro-blogging: The most successful micro-bloggers post regular content (usually a few posts a day) with some common theme or link. These bloggers are also active in re-blogging content and participating in the micro-blogging community. Traditional blogging is a much better format if you only have time to blog once a week, but you can integrate your blogging and micro-blogging with some practice.

4. Post content that is ideal for micro-blogging: Some content works very well in the micro-blog format, for example quick personal updates or thoughts, brief opinion statements, links to blog posts or news you found interesting, quick reactions to news, and event information. Those who blog regularly already may find that micro-blogging provides a great alternative to link spams or short posts whose entire point is really to highlight someone else's work.

5. Compare the various types of micro-bloggers.

- Twitter

- Tumblr

- MySay

- Hictu

- Frazr

- IRateMyDay

Blogger

Blogger is a blog-publishing service that allows multi-user blogs with time-stamped entries. It was developed by Pyra Labs, which was bought by Google in 2003. The blogs are hosted by Google and generally accessed from a subdomain of blogspot.com. Blogs can also be served from a custom domain owned by the user (like www.example.com) by using DNS facilities to direct a domain to Google's servers. A user can have up to 100 blogs per account.

Up until May 1, 2010, Blogger also allowed users to publish blogs to their own web hosting server, via FTP. All such blogs had to be changed to either use a blogspot.com subdomain, or point their own domain to Google's servers through DNS.

Available Designs

Blogger allows its users to choose from various templates and then customize them. Users may also choose to create their own templates using CSS. The new design template, known as "Dynamic View", was introduced on 31 August 2011 with Dynamic Views being introduced on 27 September 2011. It is built with AJAX, HTML5, and CSS3. The time for loading is 40 percent shorter than traditional templates, and allows user to present blog in seven different ways: classic, flipcard, magazine, mosaic, sidebar, snapshot, and timeslide. Readers still have the option to choose preferable views when the blog owner has set a default view. Some of the widgets (e.g., Labels, Profile, Link List, Subscription Links, Followers and Blog Archive etc.) are available for Dynamic Views; other templates are chosen by the blogger.

In April 2013, Blogger updated its HTML template editor that has some improvements to make it easy for the users to edit the blog's source code. The editor was updated with syntax highlight, number line and jump-to-widget button for ease of editing the code.

For over half a year dynamic views users were suffering from a bug causing custom CSS and page navigation often not to load properly. This happened because a JavaScript routine rendered the page before it was loaded. A blogger user fixed the template and published the fix.

Integration

- The Google Toolbar has a feature called "BlogThis" which allows toolbar users with Blogger accounts to post links directly to their blogs.

- "Blogger for Word" is an add-in for Microsoft Word which allows users to save a Microsoft Word document directly to a Blogger blog, as well as edit their posts both on- and offline. As of January 2007, Google says "Blogger for Word is not currently compatible with the new version of Blogger", and they state no decision has been made about supporting it with the new Blogger. However, Microsoft Office 2007 adds native support for a variety of blogging systems, including Blogger.

- Blogger supports Google's AdSense service as a way of generating revenue from running a blog.

- Blogger also started integration with Amazon Associates in December 2009, as a service to generate revenue. It was not publicly announced, but by September 2011 it appeared that all integration options had been removed and that the partnership had ended.

- Windows Live Writer, a standalone app of the Windows Live suite, publishes directly to Blogger.

- Blogger can be optionally integrated with Google+.

- Google+ comments can be integrated with blogger comments.

- The Campaigns tab in Blogger dashboard links to Adwords making it easier to create ads.

Blogger on Mobile Devices

Blogger has launched mobile applications for users with mobile devices. Users can post and edit blogs, and also share photos and links on Blogger through their mobile devices. Not only advanced mobile devices, such as smartphones, are being considered, since users can also post blogs via traditional cell phones by SMS and MMS.

The major two mobile operating systems that Blogger focuses on are Android and iOS. Blogger allow users to edit blogs anywhere through the app and either publish the blogs or save them as drafts. Quick navigation from posts and drafts is accessible from a list. Users can attach photos by taking a picture with a Blogger app or selecting pictures from their photo galleries. Sharing current locations on posts is also possible by tabbing My Location bar and adding locations. Users can also share photos and links directly to Blogger.

Blogger also provides dynamic mobile views for the blogging compatibility with mobile devices and smartphones. They enhance the readability accuracy on these smart devices, but editing a blog on the blogger app remains an open issue for the users.

Limitations

Blogger has the following limitations on content storage and bandwidth, per user account:

- Blog description: 500 characters max; Hyper Text Markup Language markup not supported.

- Number of blogs: 100 blogs per account.

- Number of labels: 5,000 unique labels per blog (an increase from the original 2,000), 20 unique labels per post (with at most 200 characters).

- Number of pictures: Ordinarily, up to 1 GB of total storage, shared with Picasa Web. If you've upgraded to Google+, your photos will be stored in Google Photos, where you have 15 GB of storage space shared with Gmail and Drive. However, if one has signed up for Google+ account, images less than 16 megapixels (4920 x 3264) would not be counted to this storage limit. For users not signed up for Google+, 800 x 800 pixels and below images would not be included in this storage space.

- Number of posts: There is no limit on the number of posts one can have in one blog. However, only 50 posts can be published per day before a user is required to go through a check process.

- Size of pages: Individual pages (the main page of a blog or archive pages) are limited to 1 MB.

- Size of pictures – If posted via Blogger Mobile, limited 250 KB per picture; posted pictures are scaled to 1600px.

- Number of pages: There is no limit on the number of pages you can have on one blog.

- Team members (those who can write to a blog) – 100 invitations per blog.

- Favicon: Any square image less than 100 KB.

- Account suspension: if a site is violating any terms of service, it may be suspended by Blogger without any notice. Repeated violations may lead to Google account suspension.

On February 18, 2010, Blogger introduced "auto-pagination", which limited the number of posts that could be displayed on each page, often causing the number of posts on the main page to be less than that specified by the user and leading to a hostile response from some users.

Private blogs are limited to only 100 members.

Support

The official support channel is the Blogger Product Forum. This online discussion forum, delivered using Google Groups, serves Blogger users of varying experience, and receives some monitoring from Google staff. "Top contributors" are community-members nominated by the Google staff who enjoy additional privileges including managing discussions and direct access to Google staff. There is likely to be a top contributor or other knowledgeable person reading the forum almost all the time.

A number of people, including some top contributors, run personal blogs where they offer advice and post information about common problems.

StackExchange's Web Applications forum has a tag for "blogger", which is used for questions about various blogging platforms, including Blogger.

How to be a Good Blogger

It's a lot of fun to blog, but it can get old fast if no one is visiting! Getting your blog to the top of the search engines for your main key phrases should be your goal to make this traffic happen. Keep in mind that it will take time, but it's very possible.

Part 1. Starting a Blog

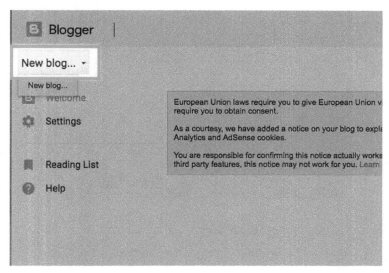

1. Start a blog: If you don't own a blog yet, you need to find the right platform for you. There are so many blogging platforms out in the market to choose from such as WordPress, Blogger, Tumblr, and Medium, Weebly etc. Try one out; if you are not satisfied with its offered features, then you can move to another, there are countless options some are free and some paid.

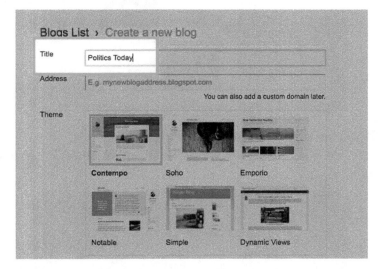

2. Pick a topic that you are passionate about: Even if you don't have a passion, writing about your daily life can make for a good read, depending how you word it. If you are going to blog about what you did today, make it interesting. People are looking for a funny story or your opinion on a debatable subject. They may not be as willing to read how you changed a lightbulb today. Using photos can help enhance the reading experience and engage readers more.

3. Read a lot: This simply means you need to go through other bloggers' posts, which helps to improve your writing skills and exposes you to new ways of writing. You must always be a student and ready to learn. You can read about topics of your interest.

Part 2. Making your Blog Easy to Find

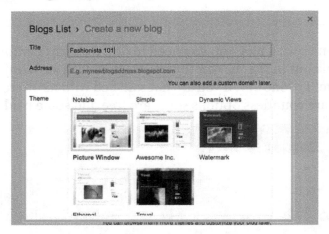

1. Design your blog: If you are blogging about fashion, travel or food, then you can choose interesting or attractive themes related to this, which helps to attract readers. Try to make a simple, stylish and professional design.

2. Learn about search engine optimization (SEO): The very basics of this is knowing which

keywords to focus on. These are what people are searching for in the search engines, and how they might find your blog. Some of these keywords get a lot more searches than others get, so it's in your best interest to eventually choose the ones that do get searched for often. Keep in mind that these are often more competitive than ones that are searched for less -- but you might get lucky.

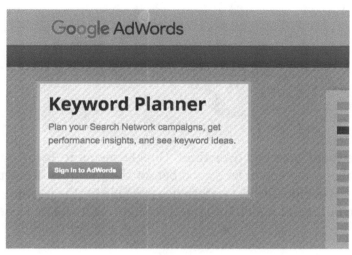

3. Focus your efforts on these keywords for now: Choose a big one that will take longer to reach, as well as three to four additional terms you're going to try to rank for. These should all be similar! Then, you're going to include these keywords in each blog post you make in various combinations. Always focus your posts on one term, and include the others only if they make sense. As you focus on these similar keywords the search engines will start to rank you more highly because your blog is tightly focused and relevant to what you're targeting.

4. Do what you can to get relevant links that point to your homepage and your individual posts: A lot of ranking decisions are based on how many backlinks you have coming into your website. You can get these links by writing articles to submit to directories, writing guest blog posts on other high traffic blogs, using social networking sites, using social bookmarking sites, and buying links (be very careful with this tactic).

Part 3. Providing Brilliant, Accessible Content

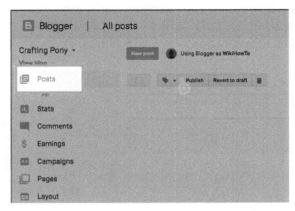

1. Show consistent, relevant postings over time: Google seems to favor domains that have had some time to age and that are going to be a good bet for their visitors. Remember -- Google's (and other engines') goal is to provide the best experience possible for the people who search with them. If your blog is going to be a good match for your search terms it will be easier for you to rank and stay there.

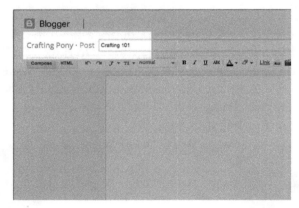

2. Stay on topic: If you are blogging about music, then don't make a post about twilight or something. If you don't stay on topic it will change what visitors think of your blog.

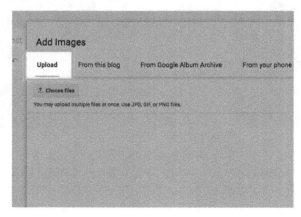

3. Make your posts unique: Make your posts something you can't get on other blogs. Try to change

your format. Also try to organize your post. The better your post is organized the better the post will seem. The better your posts seem the better your blog will seem.

- Make sure that you're always posting amazing content. The better your content and the more interesting your blog, the more people will link to it. There is nothing better than getting free links just because people liked what you have to say! Keep your mind on the SEO side of things, but also remember that you are ultimately catering to the needs of the people in your niche. If they like you, the search engines will like you.

Part 4. Promoting your Blog

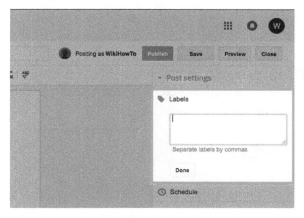

1. Promote your blog: When you start only you will know about the blog. Only start promoting your blog after you get about 15 posts or so. If you promote it before people will think your blog isn't good enough. Don't spam your link. There are plenty of ways to promote your blog.

- Use different social media platforms.

- Add tags to your post. That will make your posts show up in search engines like google.

- Add a link to your site on a forum signature. It will be better if the forum and your blog are the same topic. Make sure you post on the forum though.

- Exchange links with others sites. Make a blog roll.

2. Take a break once in a while: Don't take a break every other week though.

Part 5. Interacting with your readers

1. Be a responsive blogger: When readers leave comments, it means they're interested in interacting with you and getting your feedback. If you ignore them, there is a risk that they'll feel unappreciated and will stop reading your work.

2. When readers leave their comment on your blog post, then it's your prime duty to be responsive and get interact with them: This may show the interest of your reader on your post and also helps in building a healthy relationship with other bloggers. Always give a reply to your reader's comment, so, that they cannot feel ignored from your side.

3. Consider encouraging interaction from readers: There are many ways to do this, such as surveys, polls, quizzes and even competitions.

How to be a Professional Blogger

1. Use Google AdSense on your site to run ads: Adsense helps place contextual ads on your blog page that helps you earn money when they receive clicks. AdSense through Google requires an account and a sign-up, and it can be added directly to your website from there.

- Google analyzes the content of your blog and will post related advertisements for your readers.

- When starting a blog, consider having ads right when you start out. This way, it won't become a shock when ads appear on your blog later on.

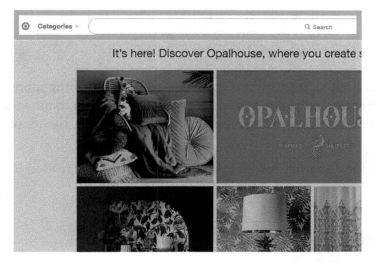

2. Link affiliates to your website to earn money per click: Recommend a product on your blog that will earn you money when people sign up using the affiliate link. You can sign up through many companies to set an affiliate link.

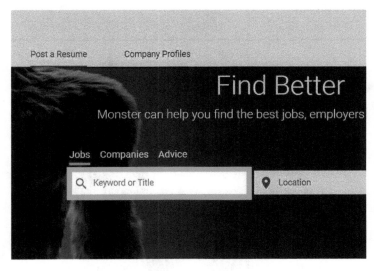

3. Consider finding a business to write blogs for: If building your own business through a personal

blog isn't right for you, search on job boards like Indeed or Monster to find businesses looking for blogging services. Many companies are looking for writers for their original content.

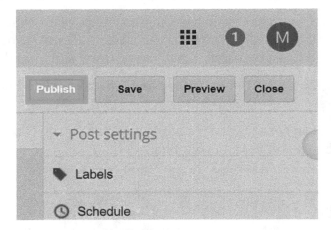

4. Know that it takes time to build an audience and revenue: Earning money on a blog is not an overnight process. Finding interested readers for your blog may take some time, so be patient and continue writing. The more content that you are able to crank out, the more eyes you may get on your blog.

- Continue working another job as you get your blog off the ground to help you stay steady with your finances.

How to Blogwalk

Blog walking is a way of navigating between blogs. If you have your own blog or website, blog walking can be a great, fun method for publicizing your site. If you don't have a site, blog walking is still a fun way to explore the internet.

Steps

1. Pick a starting blog: Ideally, this should be a site that you've visited before and know you like.

- If you have your own website, you might want to use it as your starting site.

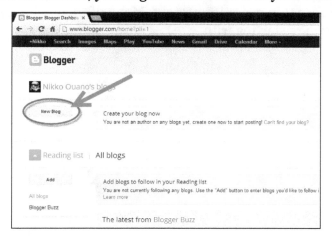

- If you don't have a good starting site in mind, do a web search on a topic you're interested in and pick a blog from the first page.

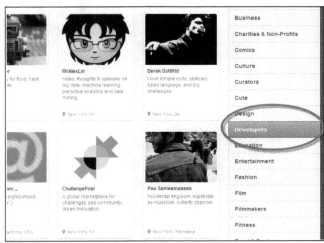

2. Find an interesting link and click on it: There are a couple of places where you can find good links:

- The site's links page or blog roll - simply a list of other blogs - will provide you with links that the site's owner thinks are interesting. Many of them will usually focus on a similar topic to the site you're starting with.

- The comments section will have links to the blogs and websites of people who read the site. The content of these links may or may not be similar to the content of the site you're looking at. If you're starting with your own blog, checking out your readers' sites is a great way to get to know your readers and to thank them for looking at your blog.

3. Read the new site: You can check out the first few posts, search for a topic that you want to read about, or just skim until you find something that suits your fancy.

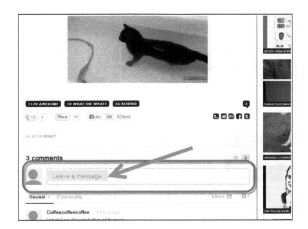

4. Leave comments on articles you found interesting.

- If you have your own blog, this is a great way to create more links to your blog and get new readers. Most blogs allow commenters to list a website in the appropriate space in the comment form. So when you comment, anyone who reads our comment will be able to click on your name and go to your site.

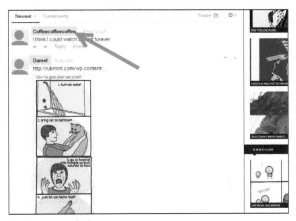

- Even if you don't have a blog, leaving comments on articles you enjoyed is a nice thing to do. It lets the author of the post know that you liked what they wrote.

5. Find an interesting link on the new site and click on it: Use the same methods described in step 2.

- If a post you liked on the current site was written by a guest poster with his or her own blog, check that blog out.

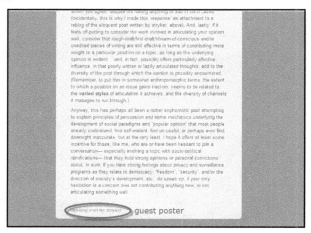

- If you read a comment that you really liked, see if the person who wrote it has his or her own site.

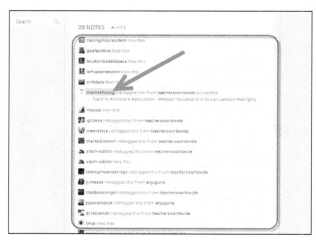

- If you hit a "dead end" - a blog with no links, blog roll, or comment links to follow, go back to the previous page you looked at and pick a new link.

Diverse Types of Blogs

Blogs can be of different types, as per the content written or delivered. Blogs may focus on a particular subject, such as travel blogs, fashion blogs, photography blogs, art blogs, etc. The diverse kinds of blogs, which are in vogue in the digital world today, have been thoroughly discussed in this chapter. It also provides a detailed explanation on the typical challenges faced by an amateur blogger and their solutions and includes ways to run a blog for a creative business, starting a vlog, etc.

Educational Blog

A blog is a publication mechanism, like a journal or bulletin. Blogs can promote open dialogue and encourage community building in which both the bloggers and commenters exchange opinions, ideas, and attitudes. Teachers can use a blog to publish instructional materials that the students can access to and where the students can make comments. Teachers can also let students set up their own blogs for a particular subject or for several subjects and then assign tasks to students. The tasks should be done using blogs (i.e., publishing articles and sharing them with other students). While the students develop their own blogs, teachers can observe and monitor the students' progress, and identify the learning needs that have not been considered (e.g., students may directly or indirectly express their doubts on blogs). As the information on students' blogs are growing, teachers need to classify, summarise and evaluate different students' blogs and then publish the teachers' opinions, directions, and feedback on their own blogs or on class blogs. By doing this, teachers are actually putting students to the right tracks, because if you just let students publish what ever they like, the use of blog could be out of control, and the relevance between the blog and the content being taught and learning will be reduced.

Examples of Blogs for Education

- eJourney with technokids is the professional blog of Anne Mirtschin. It also has great examples of the online challenges she is setting for her students. Links on the right of the page take you to other teacher and student blogs.

- Skippy is one of the students at Hawkesdale P-12 schools personal blogs. It is full of ideas, writing and fun applications such as Voki. It is also a great example of a student keeping themselves safe online by not publishing too much personal information.

- Bright Ideas by the School Library Association Victoria showcases great resources and uses of technology by Victorian Schools.

- Readers Cup - a blog also by SLAV to support the Premier's Reading Challenge.

- Connect highlights fantastic online resources for teachers and students. Use as a tool to encourage your students to 'comment' in a responsible way.

Educational Benefits of Blogging

According to educational specialists Drs. Fernette and Brock Eide, the use of blogs in an educational setting produces several benefits. These benefits include the promotion of critical and analytical thinking, increased access and exposure to quality content and a combination of solitary and social interactions with peers. The educational benefits of blogging can also extend to the administrative and teaching aspects of how a class operates.

Critical and Analytical Thinking

Peter Duffy, Educational Development Officer at The Hong Kong Polytechnic University, and Dr. Axel Bruns, Media and Communication, Creative Industries faculty member at Queensland University of Technology, suggest that students can benefit from the structure of a blog in several ways. A blog provides students with an opportunity to demonstrate critical thinking skills and to employ language and writing principles that demonstrate analytical thought and comprehension. Blogs also give students a platform from which creative risks can be taken, Duffy and Bruns say. As students are given writing assignments for blog posts, they will learn the benefits of commitment, scheduling and planning as they strive to meet deadlines and stay on topic.

Increased Exposure to Quality Content

As students apply various skills learned in the classroom to writing a blog, the chances that they will encounter scholarly material increases, say the Eides. When given a topic to write about, a student is likely to seek out data that supports her point of view. She may find content from a variety of sources and, through trial and error, will learn the difference between authoritative and non-authoritative sources. Blogging is an effective educational tool and can be used as part of the course requirements or as an extra credit endeavor. Either way, the blogs should be relevant to material covered in the classroom.

Solitary and Social Interaction

Blogs, Duffy and Bruns say, are commonly perceived as little more than an Internet message board. The educators argue, however, that unlike message boards, a blog gives its creator a predominant space to express individual views, while message boards do not. Message boards highlight a group's thoughts more than they do the thoughts expressed individually. Simply put, blogs provide a stage for a single author, while message boards provide a stage for a group of individuals. This trait makes blogging of more worth educationally, Duffy and Bruns say.

Teaching and Administrative Benefits

Duffy and Bruns say that blogging benefits students by providing supplemental support for the administrative affairs of a classroom. For instance, in addition to official written correspondence between teachers, students and parents, a blog can serve as a central location that contains material relevant to the class, such as calendars of events, assignment recaps and course syllabi. With its ability to support digital photos and videos, a blog can also be a gathering place for students to view images and video of class activities, such as a field trip.

How to Start a Book Blog

Blogging has become all the craze. There are many different types of blogs, ranging from sports blogs to cooking blogs and back again. This article will talk about book blogs and how to start your own.

Steps

1. Find a blogging site: Most book bloggers use Blogger, because it's free and the easiest. However, you can also use Wordpress, Tumblr, or any other one you find.

2. Pick a snazzy name: It doesn't necessarily have to deal with reading or books, in fact, many successful blogs have catchy names that have nothing to do with reading.

3. Design a layout: Decide how you'll place everything on your site. Will you have the picture or title of the book you're reading, and everything else to follow.

4. Create a rating system: An ideal rating system goes from one to five, however the number's entirely up to you.

5. Start reading: Make little notes about the book as you read it, if you want. Your book blog should be fun to update, not a tedious job.

6. Type the review: Start with the title, then author, your rating, and go! Begin with a summary of the book, then talk about it and describe your feelings. Finally, end with a recommendation for the book or not.

7. Spread around your book blog link: Create a blog button if you want. Make sure as many people know about as you can.

How to Create a Bilingual Blog

If you can talk and write in more than one language, have a little more time to write and would like to gain more viewers on your blog, it may be necessary to try making your blog bilingual. Not only it will get your blog more attention from people who speak in the different language, but it also helps you to improve your writing skills. Whatever the reasons, here are ways you can set up your blog if you'd like to provide content in multiple languages.

Preparing your Content

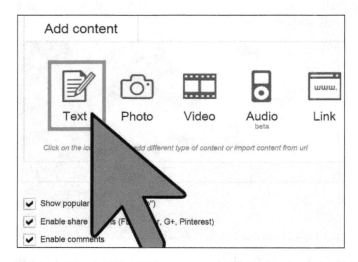

1. Write your content: Write what you'd normally write for a blog post, in the language you're most comfortable writing it in.

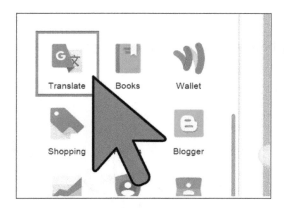

2. Translate your content: If you're able to do this yourself, that's great. If you know you'll make errors, just let readers know it's your second language and that you'll appreciate hints on improving. If you have a friend or family member who speaks the other language well, ask them to read through your translation; they may even be willing to do the translation for you but remember that you won't be able to rely on this for always, unless they partner up on the blog with you.

- How much you translate will depend on which option you opt for.

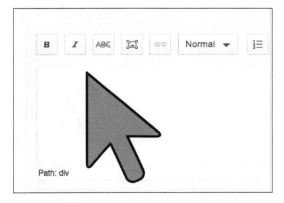

3. Be creative and flexible: In some cases, you may need to vary the translated content to account for differences in language and cultural context. Bear this in mind when translating the content.

=== Posting Your Content (Options) ===

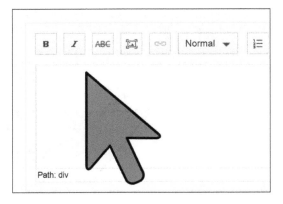

One Blog, One Post

This option lets you display both languages in the same post or page.

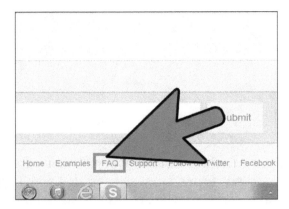

1. Write half your post in one language: Stop, then write the remainder in the other language, to complete the bottom of the post.

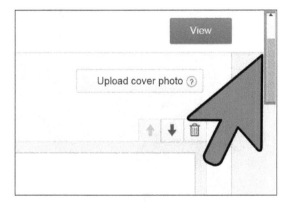

2. Set a clear line of each language: You don't want to make your readers confused, so explain why you do this somewhere in the blog's FAQs and in each blog, make a delineation of some sort. To do this latter effect, you can simply put a line between each language or you can make each language written in different format to distinguish one another. For example, language one in normal font, language two in italics.

3. Make it so that the reader will just need to scroll to read in both languages.

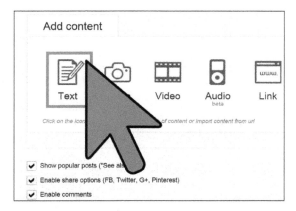

4. Include a jump page: If your post is long, you can add a "page jump" to help your readers skip ahead to their language.

One Blog, Two Posts

This option lets you have different posts or pages for each language.

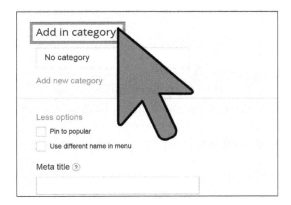

1. Create a post with language one, and then create a new post with language two.

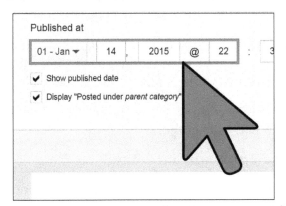

2. File posts with each language in a category: Add it on your blog sidebar to organize them and to help readers to find all posts in specific language more easily.

- You can also add a link on each post or page to send readers to the same content in the other language.

3. Schedule both content pieces to be published on the exact same date, This ensures that they'll both be up-to-date instantly and you won't end up with one out-running the other.

Travel Blogs

Travel blog is a collection of tools so that travellers can write down a journal, send the address to family and friends, set up automatic mailing lists so that every time you add a new entry to your list your friends get an automatic email. Also the theme is travel, the tools are designed to cope with you moving around, maps and flags are linked from each journal.

You want to Do it for yourself

If you want to start a travel blog and eventually become successful and making money off it, there is nothing wrong about that. In fact, it is very good to have this kind of ambition. We all have our dreams and aspirations, an idea of how we would like our lives to look in the future.

If you are an independent individual who wants to do everything on their own, this kind of career choice might be suitable for you. So, if you can't imagine your life without traveling and you would like to continue doing it in the future while making money, then this is a path you should pursue.

The important thing is to be prepared to work for yourself as well and not just dream of being a travel blogger. Work hard and you will get there.

You want to get into the Tourism Industry

A lot of people see travel blogging as an opportunity to get into the tourism industry. Although this is a viable option, there is a big mistake people make at the start. Instead of thinking about what they can offer to the industry, they immediately think about what they will get.

To get something in return, you need to give value and not the other way around. Don't be that blogger that sends emails to travel agencies asking them for free accommodation etc. Work on building your blog and focus on yourself. As you offer quality, the opportunities will arise on their own.

You want to Help others

It's good to have ambition and achieve everything you've imagined in life through travel blogging, but still, if you think that you can make it all about yourself and succeed, you are terribly wrong. Travel blogging is about engaging with various communities and sharing content, learning from each other and cooperating.

You need to establish a connection with your audience, collaborate with other bloggers and influencers, and be partners with people from the tourism industry. This means providing quality content that will teach, inspire and entertain people and be helpful to them in some way.

All bloggers need to have the motivation to share their ideas and try to bring value to people; this can sustain them even when they are not making money.

What you will be Doing as a Travel Blogger

A lot of people have misconceptions about what it means to be a blogger. For example, people think that the only thing travel bloggers do is travel around the world and get discounts and free services. If it were this easy, everyone would be doing it, but in reality, there are many tasks behind the scene that bloggers do and spend most of their time on.

You will Spend a Lot of Time in Front of your Computer

A travel blogger is a writer, editor, journalist, researcher, photographer and many other things. You will have to spend a lot of time reading about places, travel destinations, sights, landmarks, restaurants, and hotels before you can do other things. You will spend time writing, editing photos, communicating with people, booking, and maintain your blog.

Becoming a Jack of all Trades

Being independent means that you will have to do everything on your own. At least until you start making enough money to have someone assist you with the work you do. You will have to learn a bit of everything to make a serious travel blog. This includes writing, photographing, video editing, photo editing, promoting content, pitching ideas, making business connections etc.

How to Know if this is Right for you

The first essential condition for this is that you love to travel. If you are not enthusiastic about traveling, seeing new places, learning about new countries, exploring and meeting new people, then this is not a path you should pursue. Travel bloggers need to be curious and open to exploring, this is how they are able to find interesting topics to talk about and create engaging content.

A lot of people travel twice per year and think that they can easily become travel bloggers, but bear in mind that travel bloggers are constantly on the move and that they always look to find cheap accommodation and work while traveling. You need to be adjustable and have the ability to not get attached to a single place.

Traveling as a blogger is different than going on a vacation. As soon as you land somewhere, you will have to focus on your work, follow a schedule and make sure that you visit the things you planned to.

You won't have much time to sit back, relax and enjoy yourself.

There are Difficulties you need to Overcome

Travel blogging is a job and it's not easy. Like we mentioned earlier, most people only see the glamour and exotic locations, but they don't realize that there is a lot of hard work behind that. More importantly, those bloggers you look up to took several years to achieve the success they have and it didn't happen overnight. Here are a couple of real difficulties travel bloggers experience.

Competition is Fierce

A lot of people like to travel and, naturally, they also want to become travel bloggers. On top of that, they think it's easy to become one. Even though people with this kind of mindset don't create successful blogs, there are those who put in the work and build their empire carefully over a long time.

This means that there are a lot of travel blogs out there and that it is difficult to make it big unless you add something unique to what your blog has to offer.

There isn't a Fixed Salary

A lot of people are used to having a fixed monthly income on which they can rely and create plans around. When you start your career as a travel blogger this is not possible, and even later you will often earn different amounts each month. With blogging, the beginning is more of an expense than a job.

You need to invest in building up your blog and traveling to places in order to add some content to that blog. This is how things might work for a while and you will have to learn to manage with your limited finances unless you have a lot of money saved up in your bank account.

You will have to Learn how to Overcome your Writing Blocks

When you've worked out your travel blogging "gigs" and you make deals with travel agencies, you will have to create quality content on a regular basis. Simply put, you will have deadlines that you will have to meet, similarly to any other job.

Apart from having to create a lot of content, you will also have to travel and try to visit as many locations as you can while learning about them so that you can have something to offer on your blog.

You will have to become Thick-skinned

It may be very exciting to you when you start your blogging career, but soon enough you will start to understand that things don't always go as easily as you though. There are a lot of disappointments waiting for you on this path, so be prepared to try over and over again until you catch your big break.

Sometimes, you will feel like you don't know where to go next and what to try, and it is best to take a break for the day and clear your mind so that you can start over tomorrow.

Define your Travel Niche

Having a clearly defined niche is a very important thing, but at the same time, it can be very annoying. A lot of people have various interests concerning travel and they want to talk about many different things. However, this creates a problem, as you won't be able to build an audience that will keep coming back to your blog.

Simply put, if you write about various different aspects of traveling on your blog but you don't focus on anything in particular, you will end up with a lot of superficial information and nothing truly unique and valuable. Travel is a blogging niche on its own, but you can further specialize in the things you love and offer quality content.

You can find your travel niche simply by combining travel with an additional aspect and focusing on those things, for example:

- Travel and cooking
- Travel and music festivals
- Travel and ancient landmarks
- Travel and family vacations
- Travel and traditional cuisine
- Travel and fashion

These are all clear and precise travel blogging niches. Choose the one you are passionate about and where there is a clear audience hungry for more content.

A lot of people worry about whether or not they will be able to keep it interesting if they limit themselves to one niche; you will be able to do this if you are really interested in what you are writing about and if your work hard.

How to Start a Travel Blog

Travel stories, with their myriad trials, tribulations, and adventures, are made for sharing. Today, the best way to do this is by starting a travel blog. While writing your own blog seems daunting, in reality the sheer number of blogging platforms out there has made it easier than ever. With some patience and creativity, anyone can blog their adventures with ease.

Method 1. Building your Blog

1. Find a place to host your blog: There are a number of great platforms where you can build a good looking website free of charge. You can use Tumblr, Wordpress, LiveJournal, Weebly, and many others. To get an idea of which one to use, visit the site and search for "Travel." You can then peer through other travel blogs hosted on the same site and see what styles you enjoy.

- While almost all blogging sites offer a free version, the also offer paid packages that allow you to upload videos and music, host more pictures, and gain access to a wide variety of customization options. If you plan on blogging after more than one trip, you will likely need professional options.

- If you're looking to be a professional travel writer, you should consider buying your own domain name. Having a site URL like www.myadventures.wordpress.com is fine for smaller blogs, but it looks a lot less professional than www.myadventures.com.

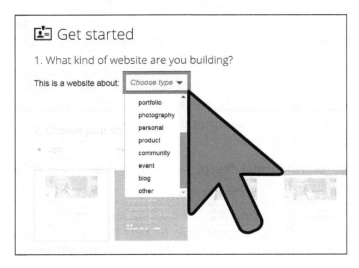

2. Think of your unique angle while traveling: What makes your blog stand out amongst the thousands of other travel blogs out there? Establish a style and stick to it. Try to pick up on a new trend

or become an authoritative guide on something people really want to know about. Think about your reasons for writing a blog - what do you want the world to know? Whatever makes you and your trip unique needs to be in your blog to be successful.

- Is your blog just meant to keep friends and family in the loop about your travels, or do you hope to reach a wider audience?

- What kind of perspective do you bring to a new place or country? Are you a foodie looking to compare different recipes. A tourist out of her element in a new culture? A photographer looking to capture something new?

- What can you teach people from your trip? Are you an inventive budgeter, a student of music or poetry, or a camping guru?

3. Think about your blog's angle when designing your page: All blogging sites come with "Templates," which are pre-made websites that allow you to focus on the content, not coding. That said, you need to choose a design that best showcases your talents and travels. Remember, you can always change this later, too, if your blog changes focus.

- Pictures: If you plan on using a lot of photos, choose a layout that offers lots of pictures on the screen at once. Many of them have a homepage or top bar with slideshows or a collage of your pictures, making them front and center for your viewers. Often, these templates show off big, high quality photos.

- Essays: Look for a very minimal design, something that is easy to read and doesn't distract viewers from the words on the page.

- Mixtures: If you plan on posting a bit of everything, consider a simple, scrolling design. These usually give small clips of pictures or text in chronological order, with the latest post up top, allowing your viewer to scroll through and get an idea of what each post is about.

4. Choose a short, memorable name: Usually, the name includes your location, but if you plan on multiple trips you should get a more general name. Puns, plays on words, and alliteration (using the same letter twice, such as "Timmy's Travels") are generally safe bets, but choose a name that speaks to you. Keep it short so that it is easily memorized and people know how to look you up.

- Try to avoid hyphens, numbers, and odd symbols or spellings whenever possible.

- For ease of memory make sure your URL and name are the same.

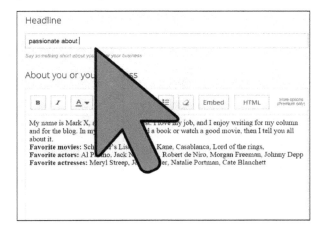

5. Plan when and how you can post while abroad, and let your reader know: Before you leave, check out your accommodations and determine when you'll be able to post something. Blogging shouldn't be the end all be all of the trip. If you're not able to post frequently or need to cut your experiences short to run to an internet cafe, you may not get the most out of your trip. However, a bit of pre-planning can save yourself the hassle:

- Know when you will have time to write, and let people know your "posting days."

- When out of service, write multiple posts. You can then schedule them all when you're back in internet range. Learning how to use your site's "Schedule Post" allows you to write many posts at once, then put them up every few days. This is perfect if you'll be leaving service again.

Method 2 Writing Great Content

1. Make an enjoyable trip your first priority: You can't write engaging, enjoyable content if you're not engaged with your trip. The best writing comes out of experience, but you can't get that experience if you're always holed up on your computer or looking through a camera lens. Set aside time for writing, but move on to other things when that time is over.

- Oftentimes, writing is best at the very end of the day, right before bed, or right when you wake up. You'll be able to reflect on the day you just had, then move on to the next one.

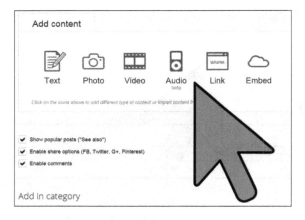

2. Brainstorm ideas for posts based on your experience, but not about you: This is the fine line of travel writing. While all of it is going to be personal (you did experience it, after all) your writing can't be so personal that it reads like a journal. You need to find ways to tackle the subjects that will illuminate or enlighten your readers. Find ways to put the viewer next to you on your adventures, making them feel like they are traveling too. For example:

- Dedicate posts to describing cultural differences, like a post on food, a post on public transportation, a post on morning rituals, etc.

- Dive deeply into one specific area, like a neighborhood, restaurant, friend you've met, or hidden location.

- Teach your readers how to do something, like how to plan their own trip, how to dress like a native, how to order at a restaurant, etc.

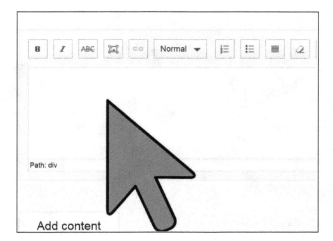

3. Write or post every few days: The more you write, the better you will get it. Even better, frequently updated sites will appear more often in search engines, and viewers are likely to keep coming back if they can be sure there will be new content waiting for them.

- Make a deadline for yourself, such as a new post every Monday, Wednesday, and Friday. Your viewers will know when to check in and you will be more likely to stick to a regular writing schedule.

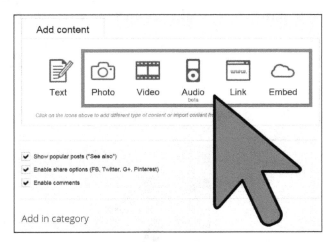

4. Diversify your posts: While you want to stay on your general theme, mixing up your posts here and there is a great way to keep your readers, and yourself, interested. If you normally write essays, post a funny personal story or a photo collage. If you're mostly focusing on food and recipes, take a day and go into a market or grocery store, or interview a cook about their method of cooking. The best part is that expanding your horizons like this will make the actual travel more enjoyable, as you'll peer into unexpected corners and cultures. Some other ideas include:

- Throw in a personal essay, explaining who you are to readers and your thoughts, once in a while.

- Teach your reader a new skill you've picked up.

- Ask a friend or new acquaintance their thoughts on your own culture.

5. Add visuals, music, and imagery: Even if you're not a great photographer, a few pictures in every article captures people's imaginations and makes them likely to stop and read. A page filled with nothing but words is intimidating, but the same content with 2-3 pictures mixed in seems much more appealing.

- Take some video of great events or post a link to a song you heard. Engage the reader as much as possible so that they feel like they're on your trip with you.

- Link out to new music you find to expand your readers boundaries.

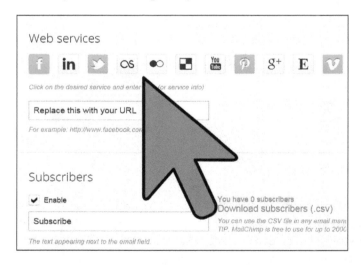

6. Use social media accounts to promote your blog: If you're a writer, send out tweets with your thoughts and links to the blogs. If you're a photographer, there is no better way to get exposure and practice than Instagram. And if you want friends and family to read, tap into your pre-made network of friends on Facebook. All blogging platforms allow you to link the posts with a little button on the right or left side (or found on the "Settings" page), which means the site will automatically post things to social media for you every time you post a blog post. Social media is your friend, and it is the best way to get your work out there.

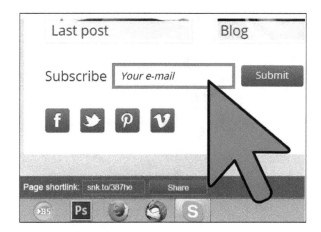

7. Comment on other related blogs: Offer to write content for them and link back to your own site. If your content is interesting enough, then you will build a fan base naturally. You might also get travel tips from others that have been there, and get ideas for new posts or topics to tackle. The best way to learn to write is to read, so pick up a few of your favorite travel blogs and start reading.

- A lot of great travel writing these days takes place in papers and magazines, like *The New York Times Travel Sections, Sunset Magazine, Outdoor Magazine,* and *National Geographic.* Go online and look up if they have covered your location for ideas on where to go and what to see.

How to Create an Art Blog

A great way to share your art with the world is to create an art blog: You can even sell artworks to people who visit your blog or offer to create custom art such as portraits for people who are interested in hiring you as an artist. In many ways, creating an art blog is just like creating any other blog except the content of the blog will consist of more images and the blog will follow a more creative theme that depicts your style of work.

Steps

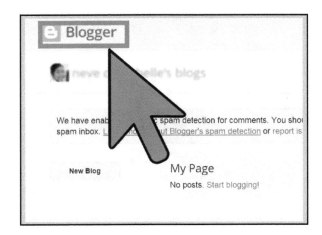

1. Sign up for a blogging service: The most popular services are Blogger and WordPress, but there are many other services available. Some of these services are completely free to use (such as Blogger) while others may require you to purchase a domain (your blog address) or pay a fee for hosting (online storage space).

2. Start creating your art blog just as you would create any other type of blog: When you use any blogging service to create the blog you will be asked to choose the following blog attributes.

- Blog URL: The URL (also known as the domain address) is the complete address of the blog, usually beginning with "(http://" http://") and ending with ".com". If you are getting a free domain address, you may be required to include a name for the blogging service that is providing the address as part of the URL. (For example, if you create your art blog with Blogger for free the URL may look like "artblog.blogspot.com" because Blogger requires that you include the word "blogspot" to indicate that you have a blog that is hosted through Blogger). Try to use the main keyword that describes your blog within the domain address.

- Blog name: Ideally, the name of your blog should match the main keyword used in your blog's domain address. For example, if your blog is about abstract art then you should include the keyword "abstract art" in the blog's name and URL. Alternately, you may want to include your name in the blog name and URL (such as "Art by Bill Joe") if the main objective of the blog is to promote yourself as an artist. It all depends on what type of art blog you want to create.

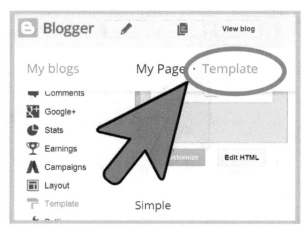

3. Pick a template: The template basically determines the design of your blog and how content should be displayed within it. The template should match the theme of your blog or the style of art that will be displayed on it. Most blogging services allow you to preview different templates to help you pick the best one for your blog. Here are some attributes included in the template.

- Font: The font refers to how the letters, numbers and punctuations will be displayed on your blog. The template specifies the font name as well as the font size and color.

- Color scheme: Each template has a color scheme that specifies the color of the background and also the color of other design elements such as the header and menu bars.

- Background image: At times you may be allowed to select a background image for your blog. If so, you can choose a background image that compliments your blog's theme but make sure it does not interfere with the readability of blog posts.

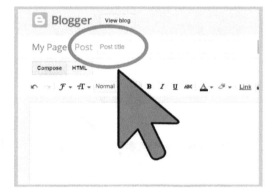

4. Start writing blog posts so people have something to read when they visit your blog. Here are some ideas to help you get started.

- Create content that is unique. Being an artist is all about being different and expressing who you are.

- Share personal stories so people can relate to your work.

- Proofread each blog post before publishing to minimize grammatical errors that may make your blog less appealing.

5. Brand your images if you want to prevent others from copying the images from your blog

and using them without your permission. Here are 2 methods of branding that you may want to consider.

- Add your signature to the images that you want to brand. Although using this method does prevent others from claiming your work as theirs, people may still try to republish your signed artwork without your permission or try to remove your signature using image-editing programs.

- Create watermarks. Watermarks are a more effective method of branding because they cover the whole canvas area occupied by the image. The watermark can be a faded texture or symbol (for example, the artist's logo) and can be made using an image-editing software such as Adobe Photoshop by creating a new top layer containing the texture or symbol and then increasing its transparency.

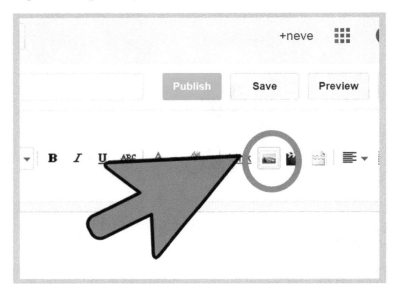

6. Add images to create an art blog that is visually stimulating: Of course, people want you to share your art on your blog or at least see your style of work. Adding images is even more crucial if you want to sell artworks or encourage people to hire you as an artist to create custom art because your customers will want to know more about the products or services that they are paying for. There are a few methods that you can use to add images.

- Upload images directly as part of your blog posts. Many blogging services display an "Add Image" link at the top when you create a new blog post. Click your mouse on the area where you want to add an image and then use the link to select and add the image.

- Create an art gallery. Websites such as Starving Artists are created in particular for artists to create galleries of their work. After signing up with such a website, you can upload images onto your gallery and add a link to your gallery page on your blog.

- Make slideshows. Websites such as Kizoa and PhotoSnack let you upload images and then choose from different themes and styles to create your slideshow. The website will also give you an HTML code that you can post within the HTML of your blog where you want the slideshow to be displayed.

How to Write a Craft Tutorial

A craft tutorial is a set of instructions for a craft project: It generally includes a step-by-step procedure for creating the craft, pictures or illustrations and helpful do's and don'ts. It is important that your tutorial is easy to read and understand, and that someone using your tutorial to make a craft can actually end up with the results your tutorial is purposed for. Follow these guidelines for how to write a craft tutorial.

Steps

HOW TO MAKE EARRING LOOPS

1. Choose a specific title for your tutorial: Your title should let readers know exactly what the tutorial is about, so you should therefore avoid using titles that are abstract, referential or metaphorical. For example, a tutorial for making ant-fabric baby bloomers should be called, "How to Make Ant-Fabric Baby Bloomers," rather than, "Ants on My Pants."

2. Explain the craft: Introduce the craft by including a clear picture of the finished product, so crafters know exactly what they will be making, and write a tutorial introduction with the following information:

- Name of the craft. Part of writing craft tutorials is coming up with descriptive, creative and relevant craft names. Use specifics about the craft that makes it stand out. For example, instead of calling the craft a jewelry box, call it a rhinestone treasure box.

- Purpose of the craft. Describe what it could be used for, who might use it and for what occasions.

- Level of difficulty. It's a good idea to include a general age range for people who would most likely be able to successfully complete the craft project, plus an estimation of the effort it takes for completion (easy, medium or hard).

- Forewarning: If, for example, your craft requires special considerations, like ventilation, high heat or power tools, mention those before outlining the craft instructions.

- List the things needed to finish the project. Your list should include tools and supplies, and should be comprehensive enough for crafters to use at the store for shopping. Provide exact amounts and measurements. Additionally, provide resources for hard to find supplies, if applicable.

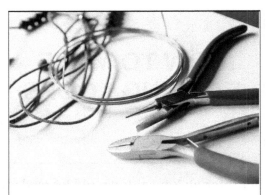

1. Thread the beads onto a head pin and cut the head pin to the desired length with wire cutters.

2. Grip the top of the head pin with the round-nosed pliers.

3. Break the craft procedure into simple steps: When you write a tutorial, follow these guidelines for creating procedure steps:

- Each step should involve only 1 action, such as, "Cut all the pattern pieces."

- Begin each step with an action verb (i.e. measure, draw, glue, etc.).

- Number the steps of your craft tutorial so they are clearly differentiated.

- Use bold and italicized font to accent important information.

- Include tips, warnings and pointers along the way, as necessary. When you write a tutorial, it helps to tell readers what mistakes you made that they can avoid, as well as useful short-cuts you learned through experience.

- Provide a picture for each step.

4. Edit your craft tutorial: Be sure to run the spelling and grammar check, as well as to read your tutorial out loud several times through in order to identify and correct any mistakes. You may also want to have someone else read it and provide feedback so that you know your tutorial makes sense logically and chronologically, and that your instructions are easy for readers to understand.

How to Start a Photography Blog

A photography blog can be a great way to show off your favorite photos as well as providing explanatory content for people following your blog. Any photographer looking to break into the business or simply hoping for viewers should consider getting a blog, which gives people a place to find your work and easily and gives you incentive to practice taking new pictures constantly.

Method 1. Building a Photo Blog

1. Consider your reasons for starting a photography blog: Are you looking to make a professional site to sell photos or are you just looking to share your work with others? This will make a big difference on your overall blog, as there are many different blogging sites depending on your needs. In general:

- Professional Photographers should strongly consider buying their own domain name (www.NicksPhotos.com, for example), so that they look like a reputable business. Most major blogging sites, like Weebly or Wordpress, allow you to buy your own domain name and customize your photos.

- Recreational Photographers often find success on larger photo sharing sites, like tumblr, where it is easy to market your work to others with similar interests. These are free and easy to set up and get running.

2. Upload 5-10 photos right when you make your site: This lets people see that you have content available right from the get go, which makes them more likely to follow your blog. It also gives you a chance to see your template (the style of your blog) in action and tweak it to fit your vision.

- Once you've chosen your blogging site, search online for "Free photography templates for _____", where the blank is Wordpress, Tumblr, etc. They are easy to copy to your own blog and many are customizable.

3. Make sure your photos are the main attraction: You want your reader's first impression to be your photography, not big blurbs of text, titles, or pleas to buy some work. Some ways to do this include:

- Choose 4-5 of your favorite photos and feature them on the top of the screen in a slideshow or photo strip.

- Make the center of your page your most recent photo or post.

- Make your home page a tiled collection of all your posts (available in certain blogging templates).

4. Add basic contact information to your page: Often this is in a little section labeled "About," but you can also delineate a "Contact Me" page on many blogging sites like Tumblr. This is important if anyone wants to use the rights to your photos or hire you for a gig.

5. Consider adding a Creative Commons license: These free licenses tell people what you will allow them to do with your photos. You can choose from a variety of options on their website, from "Everyone can use freely" to "May only be used or reproduced with permission from me." This simple addition is a great step to take in case of copyright infringement.

- You can ask people to request permission to reuse, let them know that they cannot, or can use only for non-profit reasons.

- Creative Commons has a small but helpful legal team to help you deal with disputes as well.

Method 2. Choosing Pictures

1. Decide on a theme: Having a theme for your blog makes it easier to find, easier to market, and more likely to hit it big. There are a lot of photo blogs out there, but being able to tell people specifically the types of photos they will see helps them find the photos they *want* to see, meaning your viewers will be more interested in your content. Themes don't have to be complex -- "landscapes," "portraits," and "Urban life" are all better than a random collection of photos.

- Humans of NY is one of the biggest photo blogs on the planet, and the theme is surprisingly simple and easy.

2. Post a picture every single day: In order to get viewers and build a following, you need to be constantly providing content. If you don't someone else will be there to provide a new photo for your viewers to look at.

- All blogs have scheduling features, meaning you can take 20 photos on Sunday and then schedule the blog to automatically post a new one each day of the week.

3. Add captions, stories, and personality: The best blogs are infused with the personality of the photographer. Let people know why you're interested in the shot, the weird story that happened on the way to get it, the history of the subject, or the technical feats used to make the shot look great. There are very few "wrong" ways to do this. Simply write about what interests you about the shots.

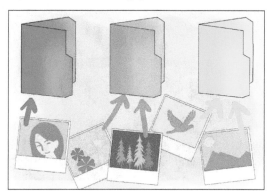

4. Consider grouping shots into "photo essays" or collections: This is a great way to bring viewers into your blog and work on your photo skills. Every few weeks, give yourself a specific challenge -- 10 photos in black and white, portraits of the neighborhood, hiking photos -- and then group those challenges into smaller sub-folders. You can even make a "tag" for the photos so that your viewers can see your many photo talents. You could have a page or group of "Nature" photos alongside your normal abstract photography, or you could try to tell the story of a day in a 10 photo "story."

5. Avoid any photos that will bring down the overall quality of your blog: While some photos might have incredible emotional appeal to you, it is not worth adding bad shots just because of your own emotions or because you didn't post yesterday. People will not respond to them as positively as you. This means using your head, not your heart, to select the images you add to your blog. Exceptions include explaining how *not* to take a shot, or an exceptional moment (such as a famous person spotted in a blur) but make sure you back it up with an incredible explanation.

- Avoid blurry images.

- Avoid boring images.

- Avoid poorly exposed images.

- Avoid commonplace images. You are aiming to be different so that people will want to follow your blog rather than someone else's.

6. Engage in the online photo community: A big part of blogging is meeting other photographers who share your interests. Follow other photographers for inspiration and take them time to let them know when you like a shot they took. Swap information on social media and re-blog someone's work if you think it is particularly impressive. This not only increases your viewership, it can lead to collaborations and future projects if you make friends with nearby photographers.

Vlog

A video blog or video log, usually shortened to vlog is a form of blog for which the medium is video, and is a form of web television. Vlog entries often combine embedded video (or a video link) with supporting text, images, and other metadata. Entries can be recorded in one take or cut into multiple parts. Vlog category is popular on the video sharing platform YouTube.

Video logs (vlogs) also often take advantage of web syndication to allow for the distribution of video over the Internet using either the RSS or Atom syndication formats, for automatic aggregation and playback on mobile devices and personal computers.

Types

Personal Vlogs

The personal vlog is an online video which records an individual to deliver information that they intend to introduce to people. The audience is not as varied as one's from corporation or organization.

Live Broadcasting Vlogs

YouTube announced a live broadcasting feature called YouTube Live in 2008. This feature was also established by other social platforms such as Instagram and Facebook.

YouTube Presence

YouTube currently ranks among the top three most-visited sites on the web. As a high traffic area for video bloggers, or *vloggers*, YouTube has created a platform for these participants to present their personal videos, which oftentimes are filmed using hand held point and shoot cameras. The popularity of vlogs in the YouTube community has risen exponentially in the past few years; out of the top 100 most subscribed YouTube channels, 17 provide vlogs as their primary style of footage. Many of these vloggers are a part of the YouTube Partner Program, which professionalizes the industry and allows for monetary gain from video production. This professionalization additionally helps increase exposure to various channels as well as creates a sense of stability within the field. Additionally, this professionalization allows content creators to be deemed a credible source by their viewers. Furthermore, many vloggers have been able to turn their channels into sustainable careers; in 2013, the highest paid vlogger brought in a minimum of $720,000 for the year. Hollywood is taking notice of this rising medium, and has placed its value ranked over other entertainment companies such as Marvel, which was recently bought out by Disney as well.

Vlogumentary

I'm Vlogging Here is a 90-minute "vlogumentary" that focuses on documenting the world of video blogging and centers on YouTube vloggers that have found success in using this medium. Starring YouTube personality Shay Carl and his family of ShayTards, this film, to be released in late 2016, follows a family whose lives have been drastically altered by vlogging, as their day-to-day lives are documented and uploaded for the world to see. Shay Carl is a co-founder of Maker Studios, a YouTube based video supplier bought out by The Walt Disney Company. The involvement of larger corporations outside of the Internet industries is a primary example of the ever-increasing need for a strong front on the digital side of one's company. This documentary is being created by a group with links to the YouTube community in hopes that it will spark interest and raise awareness of the impact that vlogging and the digital community are having on the entertainment industry.

Other

A video log created while riding a motorcycle is known as a motovlog (abbreviation of motorcycle video blog).

Miscellaneous Events

- 2005, January – Vloggercon, the first vlogger conference, is held in New York City.

- 2006, November – Irina Slutsky created and hosted The Vloggies, the first annual video blog awards.

- 2007, May and August – *The Wall Street Journal* places a grandmother on the front page of its Personal Journal section. In August 2007, she was featured on an *ABC World News Tonight* segment showing the elderly now becoming involved in the online video world.

How to Create a Video Blog

Video blogging, or Vlogging, as it has come to be known, can be an extremely daunting project for the inexperienced. However, with a bit of practice and a few pointers, you can be vlogging like a pro.

Steps

1. Decide what you will be blogging about: Will you simply be ranting? Or, do you have a specific theme in mind, such as music or sports.

2. Identify your target audience: This can help you decide how to speak and dress for your videos.

3. Buy or sort out your video production gear: Some "professional" video bloggers spend hundreds on cameras and microphones, while many people use nothing more than the video recorder function on their digital cameras. Use what you have, especially in the beginning.

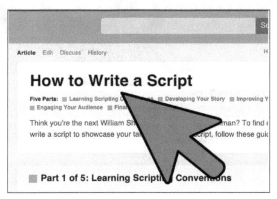

4. Write out a script of sorts for your first video: The script shouldn't be set in stone - feel free to improvise a bit while recording. Also, you should know your material well enough that the script is for learning, *not* for reading from on camera.

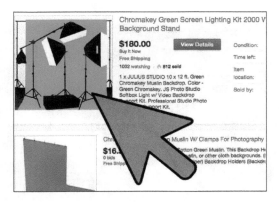

5. Prepare your video recording area: Make adjustments on lighting and the background. Some people use no background for their vlogs, while others put up a solid colored sheet to keep attention on themselves.

6. Dress for your audience: Most people don't want to see you in your holey sweats and sweaty t-shirt.

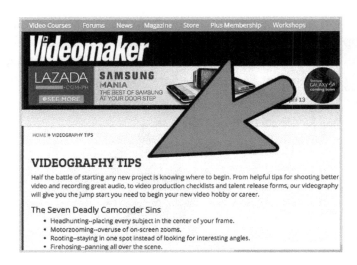

7. Begin recording: If you have a lot of gear to run, it may be necessary to ask a friend or two for help. Record several takes.

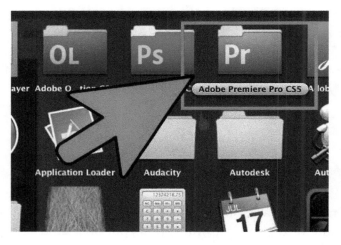

8. Run your recording material through a movie editing program: Although this is an optional step, it can greatly improve the look of your vlog. Titles, credits, music, and random effects can be added with even simple software such a the Windows Movie Maker or the Moon Valley Soft Video Blog Pack. If you have a Mac, iMovie is a great starter video editing program (it comes on every new Mac, so most people should already have it). When you're ready to go more professional and willing to spend more money, programs like Final Cut Pro are out there as well.

How to be a Vlogger

Vlogging is a fairly free, open-ended form of entertainment, but there are a few components of any successful vlogger's routine that you should use.

Part 1. Getting Started

1. Research existing vloggers: Before you create your own vlog, take a look at some existing content to get a feel for the format. Popular, high-end vloggers include people like Casey Neistat, Zoella, and Jenna Marbles, but try to find less popular vloggers as well—popular vloggers tend to have massive budgets for each vlog, so their end presentation isn't feasible for a first-time vlogger.

- Virtually every vlogger has some form of tutorial or advice on how to break into the world of vlogging.

2. Identify the type of vlogger you want to be: While vlogging is often considered to be a video summary of one's day or week, that doesn't have to be the case. You can vlog about anything you like, but common examples include the following:

- Food — "What I Eat in a Day" videos are extremely popular. As you might guess, this type of video involves showing your food preparation and final product for a day.

- Activities — If you don't have particularly eventful days, vlogging when you do something exciting (e.g., go hiking) is a feasible outlet.

- Beauty — Many vloggers have makeup- or cosmetics-based sections of their videos. If you like experimenting with different makeup looks, you can record your process as a vlog a few times per week.

3. Make sure you have the necessary equipment: Vlogging is fairly accessible in that it doesn't require a studio or intensive lighting, but you'll still need the following:

- Video camera — Anything from a smartphone to a full-blown video camera is acceptable. Make sure that your chosen video option supports HD (1080p) footage.

- Tripod — No one likes shaky footage. Buying a tripod for your camera, regardless of the camera's size, is crucial.

- Lighting — Not entirely necessary, but strongly recommended if you're filming anything indoors. A simple overhead lamp or a makeup light will usually suffice.

- Microphone — A directional microphone that attaches to your camera will pick up audio from whatever your camera is pointing at. This is optional if you're recording with a smartphone, but recommended for audio clarity's sake.

4. Figure out your intent before filming. It's important to know what you're trying to accomplish prior to pressing the "Record" button, so determine your goal for the finished product before you proceed.

- If your goal is simply to document your day, you can skip this step.

Part 2. Creating Great Content

1. Make sure you film yourself in addition to your surroundings: Your vlog should contain both commentary and content shots, so it's a good idea to get your face in the shot from time to time.

- Vlogging is personal, so you may wish to keep your vlog free of commentary and face shots. If so, just keep future vlogs consistent with this presentation.

2. Ask questions: One way to keep your audience engaged is by walking up to strangers in the street, asking a question, and filming their responses. This isn't necessary, but it's a good starting point if you don't know what to film.

- Make sure you have consent to post any responses you receive before filming them.

- Keep your questions appropriate. You don't want anyone to think you're harassing them.

3. Include interesting or exciting events: Unless your commentary is interesting enough to keep your audience engaged throughout the entire vlog, you'll need to include shots of funny, pretty, or otherwise stimulating content.

- For example, if you're filming a hike, take a few minutes of footage of wildlife, scenery, or similar.

- Including cute animals or dramatic events in your vlog will almost always keep audiences engaged.

- Wandering around any city while recording for long enough will always yield something interesting.

4. Edit your vlog: How you edit your finished vlog is up to you; however, the goal should be to cut it down to a reasonable length (e.g., between 8 and 15 minutes) while making some of the longer parts more interesting to look at.

- Jump cuts, which involve identifying two interesting, back-to-back points in the vlog and then cutting the content between them, are essential when editing vlogs.

- You'll want to add music to virtually all of your vlogs.

- Speeding up sections to create a "time-lapse" effect can keep people interested during a lull in the action.

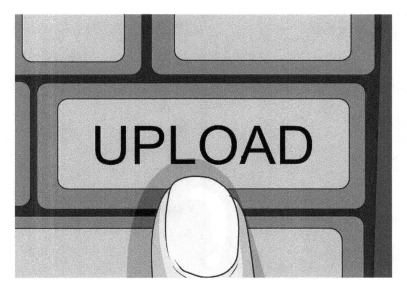

5. Upload the edited video: Where you upload your vlog is entirely up to you, though YouTube is a popular choice due to its prominence in the video community. Other choices include Facebook, Instagram, and Vimeo.

- If your vlog is over 10 minutes long, you'll need to verify your YouTube account before you can upload the vlog to YouTube.

Part 3. Engaging your Audience

1. Try to incorporate feedback into future videos: After posting your vlog, you may get some feedback from viewers. While not all feedback is useful (or actionable), pay attention if you notice a common theme among the feedback; this demonstrates that enough of the people who saw your vlog felt the same way that you should consider using their feedback in future vlogs.

- For example, if a few people mention that the music was too loud or obtrusive, try lowering the volume of music in future vlogs.

2. Create distinct vlogs every time: You can keep the same general formula for your vlog, but make sure you aren't simply copying your steps from the previous vlog.

- For example, if your last vlog involved going to a coffee shop in the afternoon and then visiting food carts, try to avoid both of these activities in the next few vlogs.

3. Establish a theme: Once you've created a few vlogs, you'll probably begin to see a trend taking shape. At this point, it's good to determine what that trend is and figure out how to continue it in future vlogs. This will ensure that the people who view your content know what to expect when you upload something, and you'll have a general framework for your content going forward.

- As with any form of expression, your vlogs will likely change over time. Knowing your general theme will help make this transition more gradual than if you're uploading without knowing what the overarching theme is.

4. Promote your vlogs: Once you have a few vlogs uploaded to your platform of choice, begin talking about them on other forms of social media (e.g., Facebook and Twitter). This is a good way to grow your vlogs' collective audience.

- An easy way to do this is by creating a Facebook page for your vlogs and then posting links to the vlogs there.

- You might even want to notify a few close friends whenever you post; if they enjoy your content, they may share it with their friends as well.

How to Start a Successful Vlog

Since famous individual, multiple-person, and family vlogs such as iJustine and SHAYTARDS began surfacing on YouTube in the year 2009 and earlier, vlogging has become an internet phenomenon. A vlog is a video blog, mostly about a person's daily life - but you can't become a vlogging sensation by just randomly posting stuff on YouTube! This article will guide you through kicking off your vlogging channel and making it a career.

Steps

1. Start with a good username: When you first create your YouTube account, you'll come across a little bar requesting your username. You may think nothing of it, go too quickly, or freak out, but either way, you need to fill this out. Make it memorable. Let's say you want to make your username EmmaSmith. week, shoot, with over a billion people on YouTube, that's taken. So you try EmmaSmith1. Darn, that's gone, too. So you get frustrated and make your username xXemmasmithaboo68958luvskittiezXx. Isn't that hard to read? It's also impossible to remember. You could have thought of something easier, like EmmaSmithLovesCats or EmmaSmithVlogging, or even just EmmaVlogs.

- Use capital letters when necessary. Capital letters separate words and make your username easy to read. Even if your username really was xXEmmaSmithaboo68958LuvsKittiesXx, those capitals added make it easier to read. That doesn't mean that username is still acceptable, though. Keep your username as short as possible.

- Cut down on Xs and numbers. They make your username harder to say and remember. You can cut down that long username to just EmmaSmithabooLuvsKitties, and now it's shorter and easier to remember.

- On that note of a short username, adding "aboo" to your name probably isn't necessary. EmmaSmithLuvsKitties is even better. You can also shorten names to another form - instead of kitties, you could use cats. So now we have EmmaSmithLuvsCats. One more thing, though - people are bound to spell out Loves rather than Luvs, so go ahead and try out EmmaSmithLovesCats. Now we have a perfect username that's short and easy to type and remember.

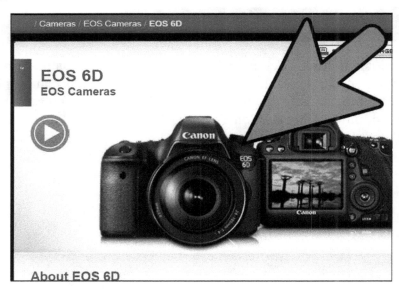

2. Your first video matters: Either get straight to the point and begin doing videos immediately, or start off with a video telling about what you'll be vlogging or a channel trailer. Make sure you have a tripod and a video recorder. Spend at least 100 dollars on a good video camera, with 720p quality or better to begin. If you have a newer iPhone, the video quality on those are great, too. Make sure you can see yourself somehow while recording, and look into the camera, not at yourself.

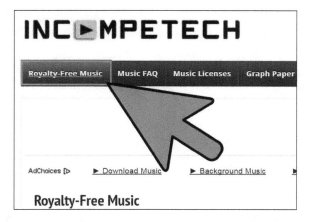

3. Use photos and music that you have permission to use: Free image websites and royalty-free music have things that you can use as long as you credit the website somewhere (for some, crediting is not necessary). Subtle background music adds a nice speak to your videos, and if you want to become a YouTube partner, you can't use stolen images or music.

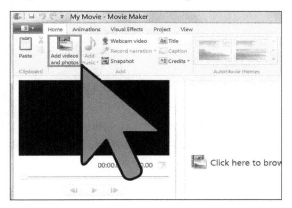

4. Edit your videos: Editing your videos adds appeal to your videos, which you'll need to grab viewers' attention. You can start off with Windows Movie Maker or iMovie, or if you're uploading on an Android device you can use the preinstalled Movie Maker. Learning to edit will also make it easier to make a channel banner, up next.

5. Get a channel banner: A channel banner is the long strip at the top of your channel's page, and it's quite boring with nothing there. If you learn to edit, you can also make a banner for your page. To

edit this, you can use Gimp for free, or buy Photoshop. Having a channel banner really adds spice to your page, which you'll want so people will keep watching. On that note, also have an avatar.

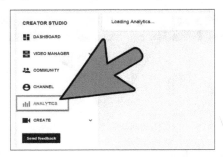

6. Once you gather some subscribers and views, apply for a YouTube partnership: This allows you to earn money from your videos. Being a YouTube partner also helps your fanbase grow. As a YouTube partner, ads will be put in your video, and you get money each time a person views that ad.

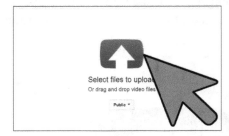

7. As a vlogger, you'll be expected to upload daily or every other day: Uploading as much as possible will make people want to subscribe, knowing that they'll get to watch something new from you often. Now you're on your way.

How to Create a Business Blog

Making and maintaining a blog for your company can be a challenging task. You need to update it every day and make the layout look nearly like your websites. So how do you do it?

Steps

1. Buy hosting and a domain if you don't already have a company website (not blog).

2. Choose the correct blogging platform needed - the best and most widely used is Wordpress. Typepad, Blogger, Movable Type, and numerous others are all available as well, so shop around and look for the one that best fits your needs.

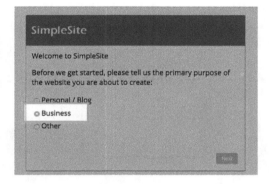

3. Develop your business marketing objectives: Develop a writing style and goal for your blog. As a business the most important aspect of your blog is that it speaks with a singular voice/personality. Your choice of writing style will reflect how readers perceive and respond to your content and (if done correctly) will establish a deeper connection to your customers.

- This personality can take many forms and for most businesses originates from their core values. If your company is fun and outgoing you may chose to WRITE KEY PHRASES IN ALL CAPS to emphasize the energy or excitement they express. you may write in all lowercase letters to identify with a younger audience that has grown up with text messaging. And so on.

4. Decide on the theme of the blog and find a template (or hire a web design company to create one) that best fits your needs.

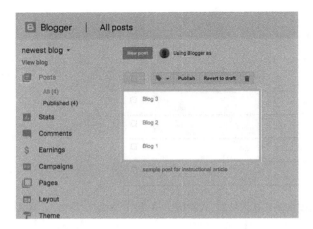

5. Determine how many blogs your company will need: It is more than 1 in about 90% of the cases. No matter how small your business.

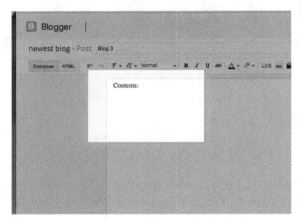

6. Decide who will be blogging and writing the content: Set realistic goals for how often your team will be able to post. Don't commit to writing once a day if you lack the time. Instead write every two days or once a week.

7. Add pictures and videos: People will get bored quickly with your business blog if it is just big blocks of text. Add images and videos so there is something on each post that will catch the eye.

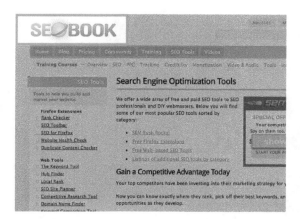

8. Use Search Engine Optimization (SEO) and have a blog promotion plan. Utilize SEO so users searching specific keywords in Google or Yahoo will find your blog easily.

9. Include subscription options. Make sure you post the RSS image icon and link where your customers can see it so they can subscribe in their feed reader. Also include an option for email, so customers can be alerted through email that there is a new post. You can also create a Facebook page where they can follow you for updates.

10. Create an About section. Most people, when visiting a blog for the first time, want to know about who is writing what they are reading. Create an About page that talks about both you and your business. Include your mission statement and the company history.

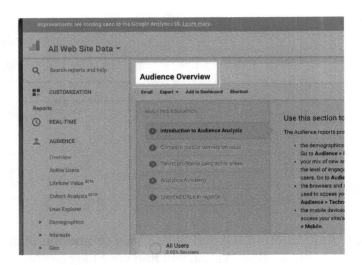

11. Be patient: Most of us won't be an overnight blogging sensation. Building a consistent stream of traffic takes time and commitment, but once its established your visitors will be a self perpetuating network of 'a friend of a friend.' Once you start you'll find that subject matter will gradually become easier.

12. Choose a consultant that will help you achieve maximum results. Ask for specifics, case studies and references.

How to use a Blog for Business

Having a blog can be a relatively cheap and painless way to promote your business through the internet. However, these days just having a blog isn't good enough. The content has to be strong, the marketing pointed, and the blog will need some care and attention if you want it to succeed. Luckily the learning curve isn't too steep and with a little help your blog can be a hugely beneficial to your business. According to research, 60 % of companies with blogs have used their tool to acquire new customers. There is no reason not to have one.

Method 1. Creating your Blog

1. Find a good blog or website creation site: You want to choose something that you feel comfortable with, so if you have experience with something like WordPress, maybe you should stick with that. Weebly, Penzu, and Squarespace are all other easy to use free blog options. Do some research and check out which one you like best.

2. Create targeted theme that stands out: You should get a palette that really helps your blog stand out and attracts visitors to your site. Try to choose one that really fits your brand. Companies that use their blog to their advantage have chosen a theme that stays true to their brand and is very targeted.

- For example if your company specializes in health food for families, make sure the tone of the theme fits that message. You won't want a jet black Halloween themed website.

3. Plan your layout: Your layout should be easy on the eyes but more importantly easy to understand.

If your reader gets lost trying to find the content they want to explore, it's going to be a huge turn off. If you decide to use advertisements, make sure they are placed on the blog in an artful way. If you have ads and content sharing the same space that can push people away from your site. You can choose a scroll down look where all your content appears on the same page or you can choose to make tabs that fit different categories. Its up to you, and whatever blog website you choose to use will guide you through it easily.

Method 2. Creating Content

1. Decide what kind of content you want to create: Your content needs to be targeted toward a specific audience, with a specific goal in mind. Otherwise it will end up being wishy-washy and all over the place. If you aren't even sure what you are writing about on your blog, how are you going to attract visitors? Take a while to plan this step.

- For example, if you are writing a blog about health food for families, you'll want to make sure that your content remains targeted. Don't start writing about health food for pro wrestlers - stick to the people you plan on marketing your blog to.

- Think about how much content you want on the blog per week, if you want varying types of material, and how this will all be produced. Having a blog is no longer good enough; the content needs to be superior too.

- Try answering common questions on your blog or teach your readers something. Above all, write for your customers rather than yourself.

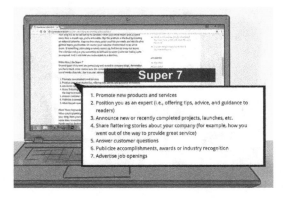

2. Follow the advice of the 'Super 7': This can be a good way to start if you're not sure what to write

about in your blog. Basically the 'Super 7' is a list of seven ways to use your blog that would be well suited to helping your business. You'll want to write as an expert, answer questions, talk about potential job openings, share new projects and any story that puts your company in a good light, and of course promote your products.

- If you ensure that you do all or most of these things on your blog the odds are it will succeed.

3. Boost Search Engine Optimization (SEO): SEO is a system in which search engines organize the websites that show up in particular searches. You want yours to be at the top of the list, and to do that you'll have to engage in search engine optimization. That means adding strong keywords throughout your blog post to make it more relevant to search engines.

- Research popular keywords in whatever industry you are a part of to help. Google Insights is a good resource if you are feeling lost. You also should submit your blog to popular search engines by visiting their search console. Submit to popular internet search sites like Google, Yahoo, and Bing.

4. Create a two-way conversation: Encourage interaction and feedback between your company and customers. Try to do the same with peers, potential customers, or really anyone who you can get to interact with your blog. The more popular it becomes and the more discourse that appears through the site, the more success your blog will have. It's all about traffic.

Method 3. Boosting Traffic

1. Start sending email blasts, sharing your blog on Facebook and other forms of social media, and asking your friends to do the same. You'll want to boost your readership in whatever way you possibly can and the first and easiest way to do this is to show your blog to people that you know. If your friends are willing to share the blog on their Facebook page, that's even better. Take advantage of whatever way you can get people to view your blog.

- The more people who visit your website starts adding up into the more that visit your business linked to that site. You can call friends, email them, share on their Facebook, whatever it takes to get in touch with them.

- Start with people you know and then grow your network from there. If you send your blog to fifty people and five people share it with all their friends, suddenly you'll find that you will get many more views.

2. Try to get indexed by Google or Yahoo: Appearing in search results is of massive importance to bring traffic to your site. Submitting your blog to popular search engines is one way to do this, as is boosting SEO which involves the use of strategic keywords. You also can look into paying for Google Ad Words, which will help your blog appear in a certain location on the search page if you are willing to spend the money. If you sign up for Google Ad Words you also get a free campaign manager for 90 days to help you market your blog.

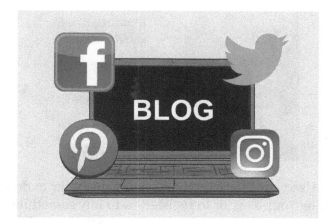

3. Integrate your blog with social media: This means making a Twitter and Facebook account for your blog. You can send all your posts to these accounts and also share other interesting posts from related topics on your page. This could start a positive cycle where you share something that someone else has written, and then they share something that you have written, and so on.

- Using the health food example, you could post interesting articles that you find about new health food research, or potential grocery shopping lists, or anything else you think of.

Method 4. Monetizing Your Blog

1. Try finding an ad hoster: Create ads for your site. An ad is a banner on the top or side of your side that markets a specific product. If you can find ads that are relevant to your business that will make it much less shocking for readers to see these ads. Normally you will need to have developed a decent amount of traffic before you can find advertisement companies that are willing to pay to feature their ads on your blog.

- Once you have built up a solid following you can try to convince advertisement agencies to promote their product on your page by approaching them directly. You can also use Google Adsense, which places targeted ads that Google generates based on search history. You will get paid for this too. You'll earn money every time someone clicks the ad links on your site.

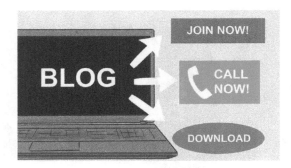

2. Create a call to action: Use your blog to convince your customer to do something with a call to action. Maybe that's sharing your blog, or to register, or to buy something, or sign up for a premium membership. Whatever your call to action is, make sure you are offering enough content for it to feel worth it to them. You need to give readers a lot before you ask for anything in return.

3. Offer paid membership programs: Once your blog has grown in popularity, you can start offering paid membership programs for premium content or special perks. Be careful not to turn people off by adding a membership program.

- The best way to do it is to keep all the existing you content you have available for free, and then when you reveal the membership plan you can roll out a ton of exciting new content only available for members. That way you don't risk pulling the rug out from under loyal readers who don't want to pay money, while at the same time enticing your readers to pay a small fee to see all the new content.

4. Search for potential partnerships: Partnerships can help boost the popularity of your blog, although you won't exactly be making money off of it.

- For example, if your blog is about health food for families you might partner with a health food store. You can help promote their services and they can help promote yours. Giving away products that the store gives you for free is one way to do this.

How to Run a Blog for your Creative Business

No matter what your creative business entails, creating a blog for it can help. It may seem like extra work, but a good blog expands the reach of your business, allowing you to talk about what you love and connect to potential customers on a personal level. To run a successful blog, host your blog online, create a graphical theme, start writing quality content, then stay in contact with your readers.

Part 1. Getting your Blog Online

1. Decide upon a domain name: The domain is the part of the blog URL that comes after the www. It is descriptive of the kind of content your blog provides and should be easy to remember. Keep the name short and try to choose a keyword. For example, if your business is about sewing, www. planetsew.com or www.diamondsew.com is an informative link.

- Keep in mind that you'll want this domain to be permanent. When you start over with a new domain, you have to start over with no ranking in search engines.

- Use a search website such as Lean Domain Search to find available domain names.

2. Find a hosting site: Your business blog needs a place to store the all of your uploads, including

images and blog posts. Some services and blog hosts, such as Wordpress, offer limited space for free. As your blog grows, you'll need more storage space. Bluehost is one such site that offers hosting services for cheap and may help you easily link your account to your actual blog.

3. Choose a blogging platform: Now you'll need somewhere to display your blog posts. Sites such as Wordpress, Blogger, and Tumblr have different features and costs. Wordpress for example is highly popular, offers the most customization options, and is free to set up, making it good for small blogs.

Part 2. Establishing Content

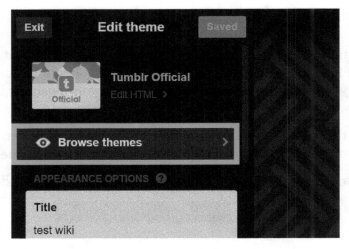

1. Design your blog's theme: A good blog must look appealing to readers. If you or someone you know has graphical and coding expertise, you can make the design yourself. Otherwise, consider buying a custom design from a site like Creative Market or using a premade one from the blogging platform. Customize it to your liking.

- The design should be easy on the eyes and allow for all images and text to be easy to read.

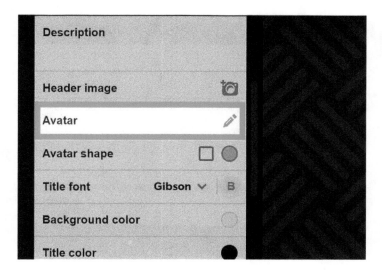

2. Add your logo: The bigger your business, the more you'll want to have a logo. It should be prominently displayed at the top of your page. This logo needs to be easily recognizable so that viewers know who you are and can identify your brand. Sketch out designs on paper before you settle on one. You can even ask your blog readers for their opinions.

- For example, a cake designer may want the logo to look colorful with a cake or frosting incorporated into it. Italic, black letters on a white background may appear sophisticated and artistic.

- Many designers make a logo out of their initials.

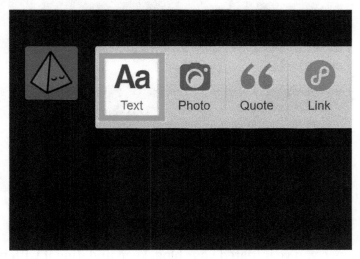

3. Create an about page: The about page will tell your readers about you. What is your business about? Why did you start this business? What experience do you have in your industry? What do you offer? It is a good idea to add a personal photo and contact information to give your business blog a personal touch. This information may also be incorporated on the front page under the blog's title.

- The personal photo can be used in the blog's header in place of a logo.

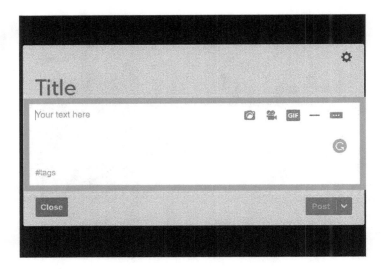

4. Write a compelling post: Once the blog is set up, it's time to initiate it. The first post you make can be a test run, simply introducing yourself and your brand, but keep in mind what you want this blog to be. Start thinking of what you want and need to talk about in your posts to make your business successful and keep your readers coming back.

- Remember to always check your posts for grammatical and spelling mistakes.

- Content for your blog might include stories that illustrate your passion for your chosen field, news about your business, and images of your products.

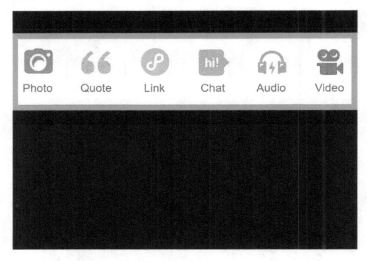

5. Add more content: Once you've initiated your blog, keep updating it with new posts. Talk about personal stories you have, such as learning your craft, your experiences opening a business, or how you developed your passion for that craft. Show pictures of your products and talk about how you made them. Talk about your values or trends in your industry. Write about business updates, promotions, news of new products, and giveaways.

- It's up to you how you update the blog, but remember that the end goal is to promote your business.

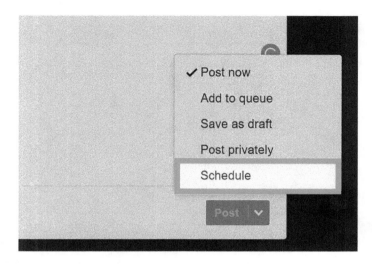

6. Set up a content schedule: In order to keep your blog fresh and at the top of search engines, you need to write content consistently. It's a good idea to keep your blog updated at least once a week. Always try to introduce topics you wish to discuss and don't forget to promote your brand by sharing yourself and your products.

- Making a content schedule may help keep you on track.

- Consistency is key to building readership, so don't delay writing until you're sure you've got the perfect topic.

Part 3. Connecting with Readers

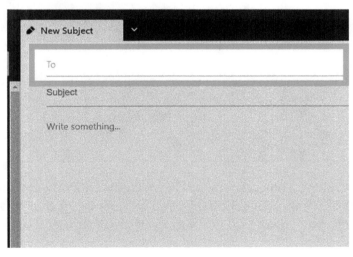

1. Start an email list: Email lists are the easiest way to gain repeat visitors. Look at your blog service for ways to do this. On Wordpress, you can install a plugin or sign up for a service such as MailChimp. Your blog should have a box that your readers use to input their email address. Once the addresses are collected, you can easily send out updates to your readers.

- It is recommended that you send your emails using a service or official email address. Mail sent through your blog may end up in the spam folder of your readers' inboxes.

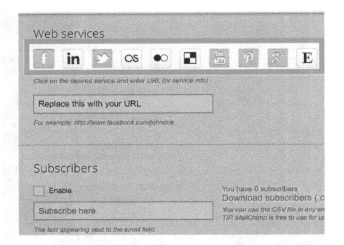

2. Promote on social media: While email lists serve as open reminders to current readers, advertisements attract new readers. Set up an account on social media sites including Facebook and Twitter. Pinterest is important since it is a site about sharing creative products.

- Social media provides an opportunity to connect with people who will be interested in your business.

- Remember to publish news of your blog posts along with a link when you update your blog.

3. Interact with your readers: Your readers will leave comments on your blogs. Take the time to respond to them in a positive way. By doing this, you can answer questions and provide more of a personal connection with your readers. They may even give you useful feedback or new ideas for your blog.

- This gives you an opportunity to build a customer base and develop relationships with people who can help your business, including other bloggers.

Creating and Using a Blogger Account

The common platforms used for the creation of blogs include Blogger and WordPress. This chapter provides a detailed understanding of the diverse aspects involved in the creation and use of a Blogger account. It includes an overview of the ways to back up the contents of a blog, delete a blog, set up a Google+ authorship for Blogger, schedule a post on Blogger, etc.

How to Log into Blogger

Blogger is an online blog publishing service owned by Google that allows users to create and manage their blogs. You need to sign in with a Google account to use it,

Steps

1. Visit Blogger.com.

2. Click Sign in at the top-right of the page.

3. Type your username or email address. If you don't have one, you can get a Google account for free.

- If your email address is john6@gmail.com, then your username is john6. If it's easier to type your entire email address in, go for it.

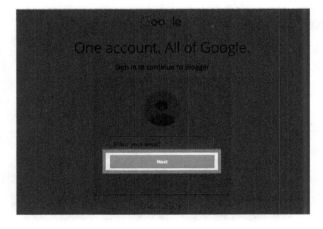

4. Press Next.

5. Type your password and press Sign in.

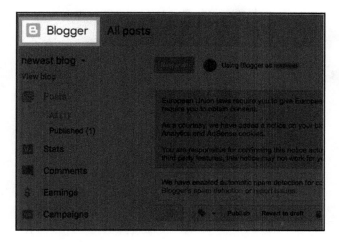

6. Use Blogger. You can start a blog if you haven't already.

How to Schedule a Post on Blogger

If you use Blogspot or Blogger to blog, you may have wondered if there is a way to schedule when your posts are published, especially when you want to head off for a few well earned days of holiday season rest. There is a very easy way to do this, following the steps outlined below.

Steps

1. Write your post normally. Then, do the following steps *before* hitting "Publish".

2. Click the "Post Options" link above the Publish button. This will allow you to change the options for reader comments, HTML settings, and publish scheduling.

3. Change the "Post date and time" option to "Scheduled at".

- Change the date and time to your desired post time.

4. Press "Publish post": At this point, your blog post will go into a queue and will not appear until the scheduled date and time. You can add as many blog posts to the queue as wished.

5. Keep tabs on your scheduling: You can rely on the Blogger list itself (scheduled posts are clearly shown, see image example) so that you know which blog posts are coming up and which have already been published. If you need to update anything before it is scheduled to appear, you'll be able to locate it quickly and make changes.

- If you're scheduling because you're going away, it is helpful to alert your readers to the fact that you're scheduling for holiday reasons in case they wonder why you're not responding to their comments.

How to Delete a Blog on Blogger

You may want to do so if you're no longer using or interested in a blog that you own.

Method 1. Deleting Your Entire Blog

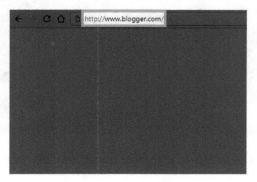

1. Go to Blogger: If you're not automatically logged in, click on Sign In in the upper right, and enter your Google username and password.

- The window will open to the main screen of your most-recently accessed blog.

2. Click on ▼. It's located to the right of your blog's title, just below the Blogger logo in the upper left of the window.

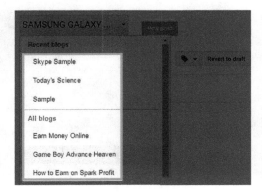

3. Click on the blog you wish to delete. All of your Blogger blogs will appear in the drop-down you just opened.

- Only owners or admins can delete a blog.

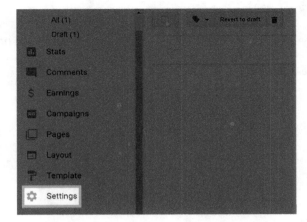

4. Click on Settings: It's near the bottom of the menu on the left side of the window.

- You may have to scroll down to see it.

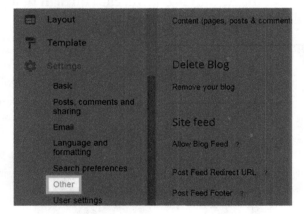

5. Click on Other: It's near the bottom of the sub-menu that opens under Settings.

6. Click on Delete Blog: It's on the right side of the screen, in the second section of options.

- If you want to save a copy of your blog, click Download Blog in the dialog box that pops up.

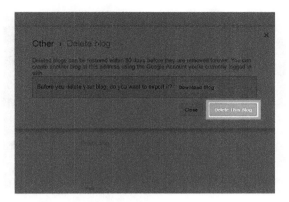

7. Click on Delete This Blog: Your blog has been deleted from your Blogger account.

- You'll have 90 days to change your mind and restore the blog. You can do so from the De-leted Blogs list in the drop-down menu of your Blogger blogs.

Method 2. Deleting Specific Posts

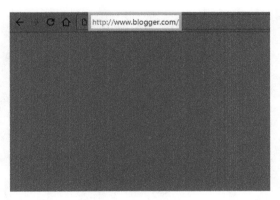

1. Go to Blogger: If you're not automatically logged in, click on Sign In in the upper right, and enter your Google username and password.

- The window will open to the main screen of your most-recently accessed blog.

2. Click on ▼. It's located to the right of your blog's title, just below the Blogger logo in the upper left of the window.

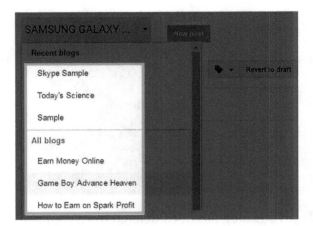

3. Click on the blog containing the post you wish to delete. All of your Blogger blogs will appear in the drop-down you just opened.

- Only owners or admins can delete a blog post.

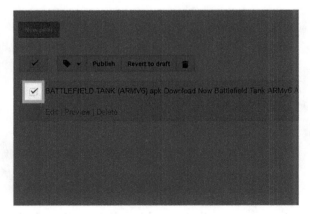

4. Check the blog post you wish to delete. All the posts in your blog will appear on the right side of the screen.

- You may need to scroll down to find the post you want to delete.

5. Click on Delete: It will appear just beneath the checked post.

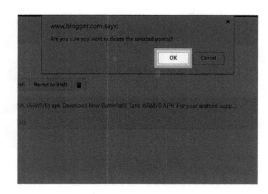

6. Click on OK: The deleted post will no longer appear in your blog and any existing links to it will no longer function.

How to Automate Blogger Blogs

Want blogs you can set up and forget? Impossible with Blogger? Not really. Use free tools available online to automate Blogger and increase your niche profits.

Steps

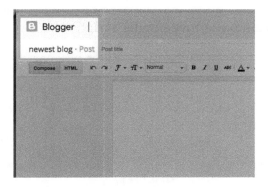

1. Create a Blogger blog if you don't already have one.

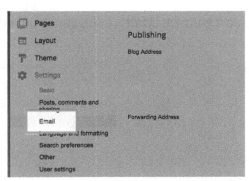

2. Go to your Blogger dashboard and click on settings, then email.

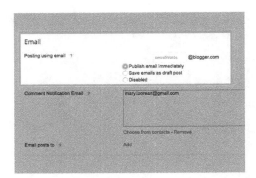

3. Under Email, you will find a section called Mail to blogger address. Create a special email address. All emails received at this address are automatically turned into blogger blog posts.

4. Go ahead and download a simple autoresponder script.

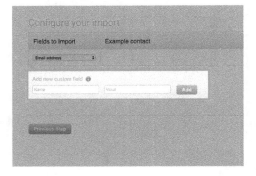

5. In the autoresponder script, add your the Mail to Blogger email address as a subscriber.

6. Add all the unique, quality articles that you plan to post on your blog and set up the interval at which you would like them to appear.

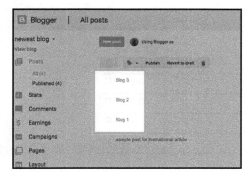

7. Test it out.

How to Set up Google+ Authorship for Blogger

A crucial factor in getting a better Google pagerank for your website is Google+ authorship. Since Google owns Blogger, setting up Google+ authorship is easy.

Steps

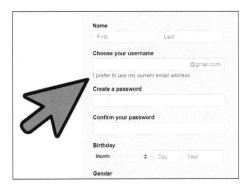

1. Create a Google+ account, if you don't already have one.

2. Log into your Blogger dashboard.

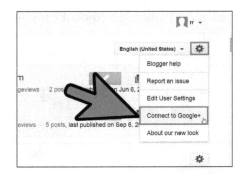

3. Click the settings button on the top right and click on Connect To Google+ in the submenu that appears.

4. Tick the checkbox and click the Switch Now button.

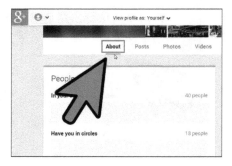

5. Go to the about page of your Google+ profile.

6.In the about page, find the links section. Then click edit.

7. In the Contributor To subsection, add your blog's URL and title and click done.

8. To confirm your changes, go to the Google rich snippets testing tool.

How to Remove the Custom Domain from a Blogger Blog

There are lots of people who first get their own domain to host their blog on Blogger. However, if they don't get much money to pay yearly subscription, they don't renew that, and also can't take advantage of their old posts. Those old posts may get visitors in future, and may earn them because they can't remove the domain. So, here are the clear steps to remove your custom domain and continue to Blogspot.

Steps

1. Open the Blogger Dashboard of the blog.

2. Click on "Settings" in Basic tab.

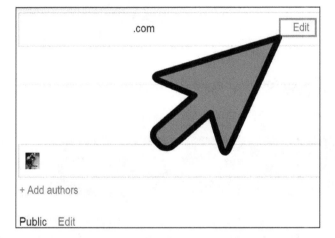

3. However your mouse's cursor over your blog address bar when the page is finished opening.

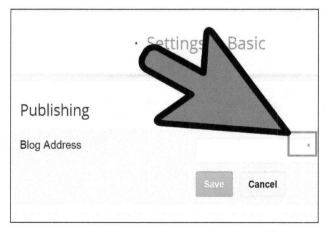

4. Look for the X icon and click that.

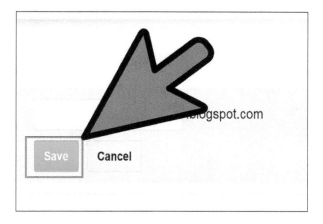

5. Wait for a confirmation dialog box to appear. When you see that, click "Remove".

How to Back up your Blogger Contents

If you're worried about losing your Blogger, or want to post your contents elsewhere or repost it on a new blog, you can easily save your Blogger contents on your computer. The process for backing it up is easy.

Steps

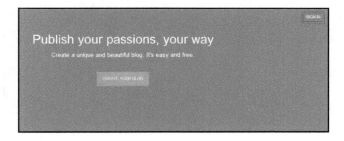

1. Sign in to Blogger. Go to blogger.com and sign in with your email address.

2. Click on the Settings option from the side bar.

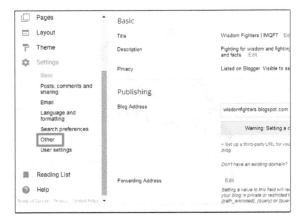

3. Select Other from the settings list.

4. Back up your contents. Just click on the Back up content to do that.

5. Download the backup file. Click on the Save to your computer button to download it.

6. Restore your content using your backup. If you want to restore your data, just click on Import content and import the backup file from your computer.

WordPress : A Blogging Platform

WordPress is an open-source and free content management system, which is based on PHP and MySQL. Some of its key features are a plugin architecture and template system. WordPress is perhaps the most popular website management globally. The chapter closely examines the key aspects of blogging in WordPress, such as creating a WordPress blog, creating a page on WordPress blog, adding a new post in WordPress and adding or deleting a WordPress post, etc. to provide an extensive understanding of this blogging platform.

How to Create a WordPress Blog

Creating a WordPress blog is a quick and easy way to get started posting your writing online and building your name in the blogosphere. You can create a WordPress blog for free through the WordPress website if you don't have your own webhost, or you can upload the WordPress files to your own domain and create your blog from scratch. Follow this guide to learn how to create your blog in a few short minutes.

Method 1. Creating a WordPress-Hosted Blog

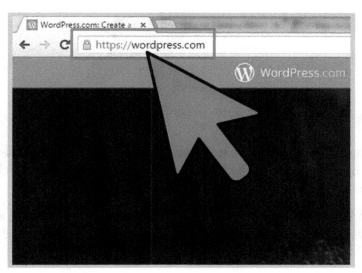

1. Decide if WordPress-hosting is right for you: If you'd like a place to post your content online, then a WordPress.com account may be what you are looking for. WordPress does all of the coding and hosting, and all you have to do is upload your content.

- You cannot make money from ads if you use WordPress.com. If you want to run your ads on your blog, you'll need to host the site yourself. See the following section for details.

2. Create an account: You will need to enter a valid email address, create a username and password, and come up with your blog's web address. If you want to create a free blog, your site name will be <yoursitename>.wordpress.com.

- You can choose more direct URLs for a yearly fee, including .com, .net, .org, and more. The process varies depending on the extension you want.

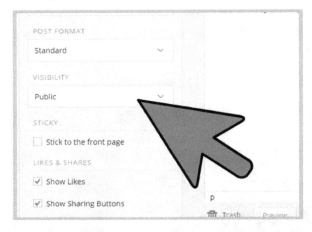

3. Choose your settings: Once you've created your account, you will be taken to your new blog's Dashboard. This is where you control the look and feel of your new blog. Click the Settings button in the left menu of the Dashboard.

- Set your title: Your Site Title is what appears at the top of your blog and in the title bar of the web browser. Set the title to whatever you want. Changing your title will not change your blog's address.

- Set your tagline: A tagline is a quick description of your blog. Some themes will display it beneath the title, and some browsers will list it in the title bar after the title.

- Set your email: The email address you list is where all of your comment moderation emails are sent to.

- Set your blog's timezone: The default timezone is for London, so set the timezone to your local time.

- Set your date and time format: The date and time format will change the way the date and time is displayed next to your blog posts and comments.

4. Change the theme: By default, your blog will use the standard WordPress theme. You can change the theme by clicking the Appearance menu in your Dashboard and then selecting Themes. You can browse through a large selection of themes that are available to install on your blog for free or for purchase.

5. Customize the theme: Once you have a theme picked out, you can customize it by clicking the Customize button in the Themes section of the Dashboard. Here you can change the colors, header images, backgrounds, and more.

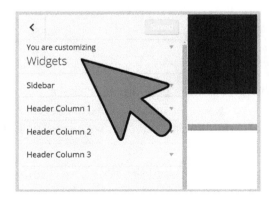

6. Add widgets: Widgets allow you to add tools to your sidebar that connect to information from

other sources. For example, you can include a Twitter widget which will show all of your recent Twitter posts in your WordPress blog.

- Click Appearance in your Dashboard and select Widgets. Drag the widget that you want to install from the Available widgets section to the portion of your blog that you want it to appear. Click the arrow button next to the widget to open its configuration options.

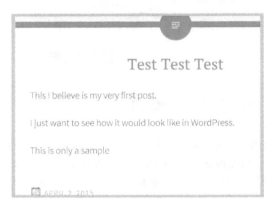

7. Create your first post: Open your Dashboard and select the Posts option from the menu. Click the Add New button to open the post creation screen.

- Give your post a title that catches the eye and invites the reader in.

- Write a welcome post to open your blog. Let readers know what you intend to accomplish by writing a blog, and any plans you have for content.

Method 2. Hosting Your Own WordPress Blog

1. Decide if you want to host the blog yourself: You can create a WordPress blog in two different ways. If you have a hosting service, you can install WordPress through your webhost and have complete control over your blog. If you'd rather not deal with hosting and configuring the blog, you can have WordPress host it for you.

- If you have your own host, you can install the WordPress software for free.

- If you want to run ads on your blog, you will need to host it yourself. This is also true if you want to install custom themes or manually adjust the blog's code.

2. Find a host that supports WordPress: A webhost is your website's server, and contains all of the data for your website. Several of the most popular webhosting services provide WordPress preinstalled, or allow easy installation. These include, but are not limited to:

- HostGator
- DreamHost
- Go Daddy

3. Login to your control panel: Most webhosts provide customers with a control panel (cPanel) that allows you to control the operation of your website.

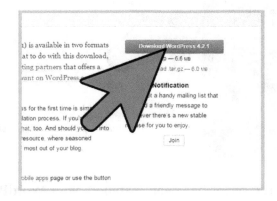

4. Install the WordPress script. Most webhosts will have WordPress already loaded and ready to

install. Simply scroll down on your cPanel and look for the WordPress installation link. This is usually located in the Scripts category.

- You will be asked to create an admin username and password for your blog.

HOSTING GATEWAY

USERNAME OR CUSTOMER #   I forgot

PASSWORD   I forgot

LOG IN   CREATE AN ACCOUNT

5. Upload the WordPress script. If your webhost does not provide WordPress preinstalled, you will need to upload it to your webserver. To do this, download the script from the WordPress.org website.

- Connect to your webhost via FTP. Upload the WordPress files to the root of your domain. If you want WordPress to exist in a subdomain on your site, create the folder for the subdomain and place the WordPress files in that folder.

- Open the webpage where you uploaded the WordPress files to. You will see an option to run the installation script. Click the link and WordPress will install itself.

6. Log in to your blog. Once the script has been installed, your WordPress blog is ready to use. Open the blog in your web browser, and log in with your administrator information. This will take you to your Dashboard, where you will be able to control all of the aspects of your blog.

7. Create your first post: Click the New button at the top of the page to open the post creation window. Here you can create your first post, introducing yourself and your blog.

- Add a title that stands out and makes the reader want to read your whole post.

Method 3. Creating a Successful Blog

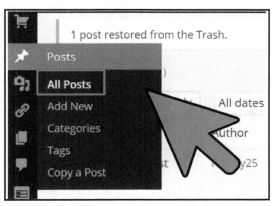

1. Post often: A good blog sticks to a consistent release schedule for new content. This keeps readers coming back to your site on a regular basis. Try to not keep your readers waiting for content to come.

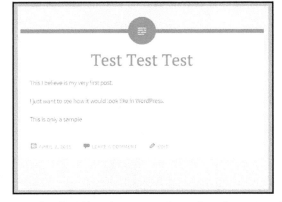

2. Keep it short: The average reader's attention span is quite short. Make sure that your blog posts

don't ramble on, and that you get all of your important information out quickly. Try to keep posts between 250-1000 words.

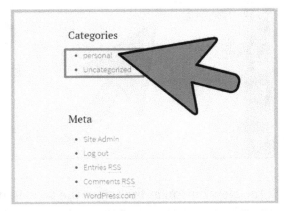

3. Be unique: Create a blog that stands out from the rest. Address a niche audience that doesn't have any other outlet for what you're discussing. If you're writing to an audience that has a lot of other options, make sure that the quality of your posts is better than most.

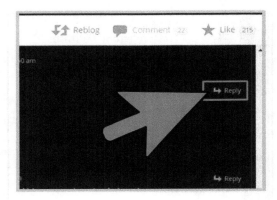

4. Interact with your readers: Respond to their tweets and emails. Answer any good questions in your comments. Make your readers feel at home on your blog, and they will keep coming back.

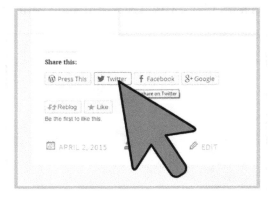

5. Promote your blog: There are a variety of ways to increase readership to your blog, including advertising on social networks, commenting on other blogs, playing around with SEO (Search Engine Optimization), and more. Experiment with ways to get your blog out there and circulating.

How to Create a Page on your WordPress Blog

In the 'blog world', there are blogs posts and there are pages. Posts go to your blog's home page in reverse chronological order and pages might hold content like 'Contact Me', 'About Me', 'Copyright Information', etc. This article will show you how to create a page.

Steps

1. Go to your WordPress Dashboard: You will need to go to your blog and log in as an admin.

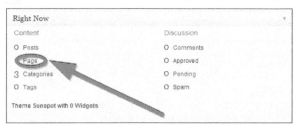

2. Click on 'Page' or 'Pages'. Either one will take you to the same place.

- With this screenshot, you can see the initial view that you will see when you first go to the page.

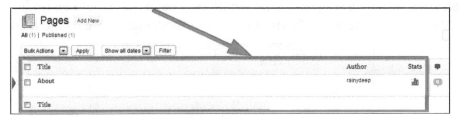

3. Click on the 'Edit' button underneath 'About' so that you can edit the page. This is a good place to let others know about you.

4. Add a new page: On the sidebar, you will see under, 'Pages', 'Add New'. Click on that to add a new page.

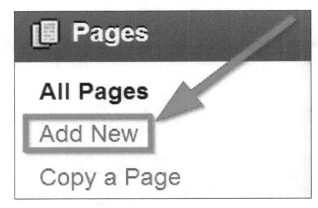

- This will bring you to a new edit box for creating your new page for your blog.

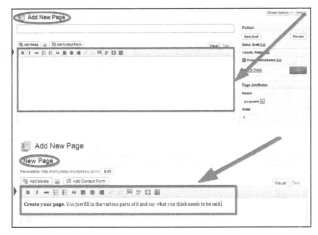

5. Create your page: You just fill in the various parts of it and say what you think needs to be said.

6. Decide if you want it to be a subpage: That would be a page that would go under a parent page. Like if under 'About Me', there was 'My Hobbies', 'My Likes', etc., those would be the subpages.

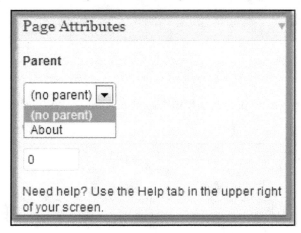

7. Publish: Once you have finished, click on Publish and it will be part of your site.

How to Add a New Post in Wordpress

WordPress is a popular blogging platform that was created in 2003 and has since grown to include millions of users. Its template system allows bloggers to choose a theme for their blog and submit their content using forms. This is a user-friendly and efficient system for writing blogs. Users can add posts from different computers by simply signing into their WordPress account. Smart phone users can also download WordPress applications that allow them to post to their blog when they are away from a computer. Consistently updating a blog with new posts is the best way to encourage people to read your blog. This article will show you how to add a new post in WordPress.

Steps

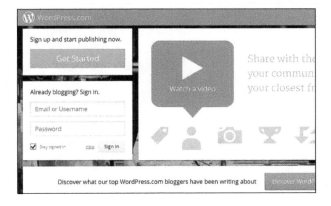

1. Sign into your WordPress blog.

- If you do not have a WordPress blog, go to the WordPress home page and click on the orange button that says "Get Started Here." It will take you through the sign up process.

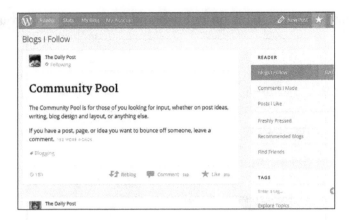

2. Click on "My Account" on the left side of the tool bar at the top of the page.

3. Scroll down your dashboard: Your dashboard is the list on the left side of the page. Click on the small arrow to the right of the "Posts" Tab. This will show you options for your posts, including "All Posts," "Add New," "Categories," "Post Tags" and "Copy a Post."

4. Click "Add New." This will take you to your "Add New Post" page and allow you to blog.

- You can also click the "New Post" button at the top of your page. There should be a horizontal bar that lists your website URL. The button is on the right side of this bar.

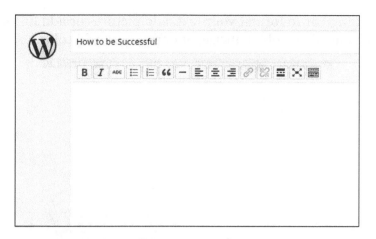

5. Enter a title in the first line of the form: Call your post something that will interest people and help them identify the content.

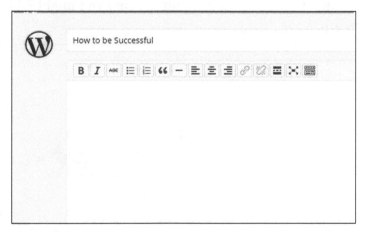

6. Move your cursor down to the text box below the title and start to write your post. The post will appear differently depending upon the theme you have chosen.

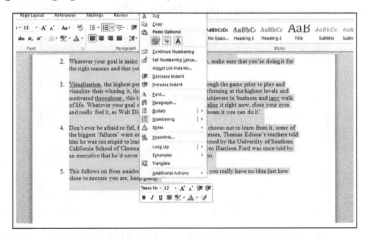

7. You can also cut and paste it from a word processor: Use the button on your formatting tool bar to paste. Click on the folder with a "T" on it to paste text.

- Use the formatting bar to format your text, add pictures or add links. The formatting bar includes options to align, bold, italicize, underline and add color.

8. Add tags to your post by writing in the subjects that your post covers: Type in a word or phrase and press "Add." For example, if your post is about cooking you might add "Chocolate" or "Zucchini" as tags.

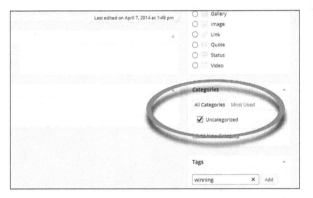

9. Organize your post by adding categories: The "Categories" box is right below the "Tags" box. Add categories that express the overall themes and interests of your post. If your post is about cooking, you would add "Cooking" and perhaps "Culinary" as categories.

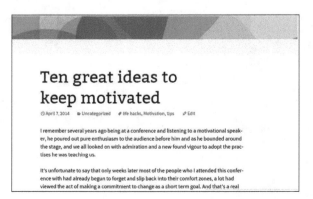

10. Preview your post before publishing it to your blog: The "Preview" button is to the right and above the "Publish" button to the right of your post. Return to the post to edit it, if you want to make any changes.

- If you need to stop at any point, click "Save Draft" in order to keep the post as a draft rather than publish it.

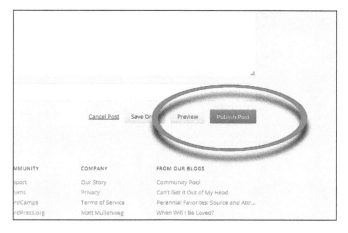

11. Publish your new WordPress post by clicking "Publish."

How to Delete a WordPress Post

Method 1. Temporarily Deleting a Post

1. Go to wordpress.com and sign in with your account.

2. Open your dashboard by clicking on the My Site button.

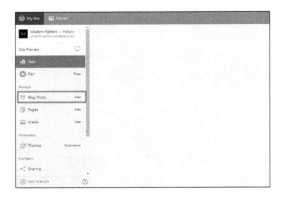

3. Select Blog Posts from the sidebar to open the blog posts menu.

4. Select a post. Click on the More button.

5. Click on the Trash button to delete the post. Done.

Method 2. Permanently Deleting a Post

1. Go to Trash: Click on the Trashed option from the Blog Posts menu.

2. Select the post you want to permanently delete. Click on Delete Permanently.

3. Done: Now your post is permanently deleted.

How to Delete a WordPress.Com Blog

You can do this on both the mobile and the desktop versions of WordPress. Once you delete your WordPress blog, you cannot retrieve it. Keep in mind that some archived versions of your blog will remain searchable on Google for several days to several weeks following the blog deletion. If you just want to delete a post on your WordPress site, you can do that instead.

Method 1. Deleting an Entire Site on Desktop

1. Open the WordPress website: Go to https://wordpress.com/. This will open your WordPress dashboard if you're already logged in.

- If you aren't already logged in, click Log In in the top-right side of the page, then enter your email address and password.

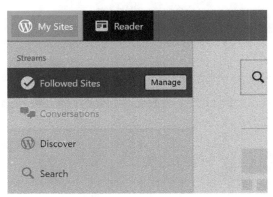

2. Click My Sites: It's in the top-left corner of the page. A pop-out menu will appear.

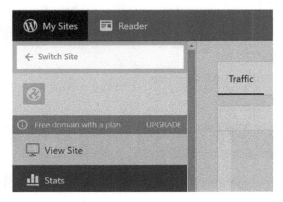

3. Make sure you're on the correct blog: If you have multiple blog titles on one email account, click Switch Site in the upper-left corner of the pop-out menu, then click the title of the blog that you want to delete.

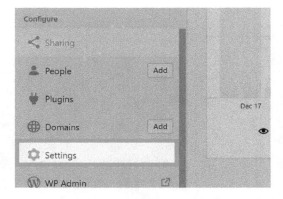

4. croll down and click Settings: It's toward the bottom of the pop-out menu. Doing so will open the Settings page.

- Your mouse must be hovering over the pop-out menu in order to scroll down to Settings.

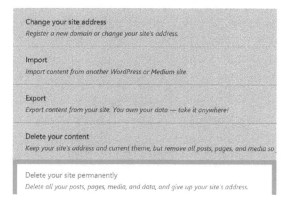

5. Scroll down and click Delete your site permanently. This is the red-text option at the very bottom of the page.

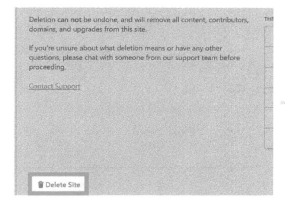

6. Scroll down and click Delete Site. It's at the bottom of the page.

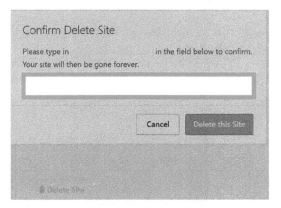

7. Enter your site's web address when prompted: Click the text field in the middle of the pop-up window, then type in the full address for your blog as indicated by the text at the top of the pop-up window.

- For example, if your blog was named "ilovehuskies.wordpress.com", that's what you would enter in this text field.

8. Click Delete this Site: This red button is in the lower-right corner of the window. Clicking it will delete your blog and make available the blog's address.

- It may take several days for the blog to disappear from Google archive pages.

Method 2. Deleting an Entire Site on Mobile

1. Open WordPress: Tap the WordPress app icon, which resembles the WordPress "W" logo. This will open your WordPress dashboard if you're logged in.

- If you aren't logged in, enter your email address and password to continue.

2. Tap the WordPress icon: On iPhone it's in the bottom-left corner of the screen and on Android it's on the top-left of the screen. Doing so will bring up your main WordPress blog's dashboard.

3. Make sure that you're on the correct blog. If you have more than one blog under the same email address, tap Switch Site in the top-left corner of the screen, then tap the name of the blog that you want to delete.

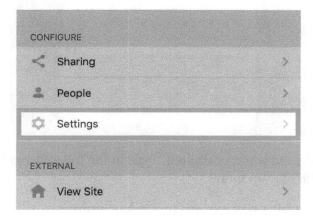

4. Scroll down and tap Settings. This gear-shaped icon is near the bottom of the page.

5. Scroll down and tap Delete Site. It's at the bottom of the Settings page.

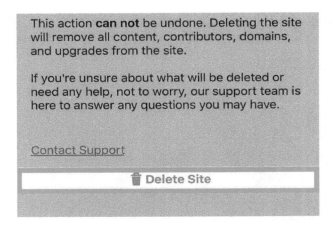

6. Tap Delete Site (iPhone) or YES (Android). Doing so takes you to the confirmation page.

7. Enter your site's web address when prompted. Type in the full address for your blog as indicated by the text at the top of the pop-up menu.

- For example, if your blog was named "pickledcucumbers.wordpress.com", you would type pickledcucumbers.wordpress.com into the text field.

8. Tap Permanently Delete Site: It's the red text below the text field. Tapping this option permanently deletes your blog from WordPress.

- On Android, you'll just tap DELETE here.
- It may take several days for the blog to disappear from Google archive pages.

Method 3. Deleting a Single Post on Desktop

1. Open the WordPress website: Go to https://wordpress.com/. This will open your WordPress dashboard if you're already logged in.

- If you aren't already logged in, click Log In in the top-right side of the page, then enter your email address and password.

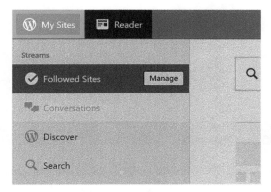

2. Click My Sites: It's in the top-left corner of the page. A pop-out menu will appear.

3. Make sure you're on the correct blog: If you have multiple blog titles on one email account, click

Switch Site in the upper-left corner of the pop-out menu, then click the title of the blog that you want to delete.

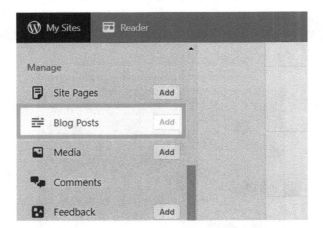

4. Click Blog Posts. It's an option under the "Manage" heading in the left-hand column.

5. Find the post you want to delete. Scroll down until you find the post in question.

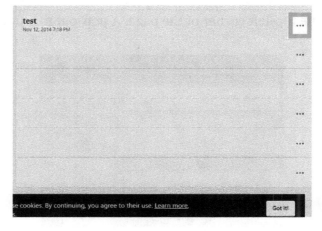

6. Click. This option is to the right of the post. A drop-down menu will appear.

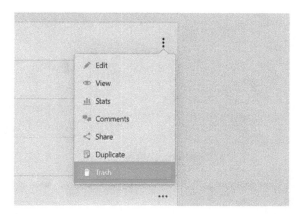

7. Click Trash: It's in the drop-down menu. Doing so immediately deletes the WordPress post.

Method 4. Deleting a Single Post on Mobile

1. Open WordPress: Tap the WordPress app icon, which resembles the WordPress "W" logo. This will open your WordPress dashboard if you're logged in.

- If you aren't logged in, enter your email address and password to continue.

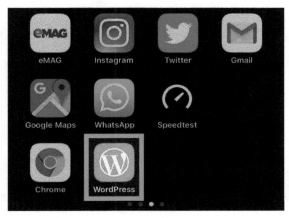

2. Tap the WordPress icon: On iPhone it's in the bottom-left corner of the screen and on Android it's on the top-left of the screen. Doing so will bring up your main WordPress blog's dashboard.

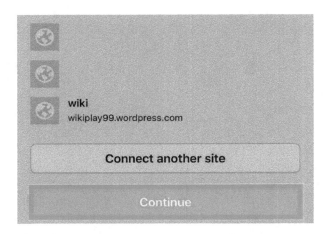

3. Make sure that you're on the correct blog: If you have more than one blog under the same email address, tap Switch Site in the top-left corner of the screen, then tap the name of the blog that you want to delete.

4. Tap Blog Posts: You'll find it in the "PUBLISH" section.

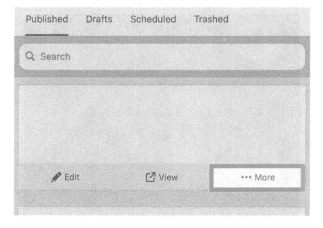

5. Tap More: It's below the bottom-right corner of the post.

- Skip this step on Android.

6. Tap Trash. This is below the post.

7. Tap Move to Trash when prompted. Doing so deletes the post from your WordPress site.

- On Android, tap DELETE when prompted.

Designing a Blog

Blogs can attract an audience if it is unique, attractive and completely functional. The design of a blog is the next crucial thing after the quality of content. This chapter has been carefully written to provide an insight into the designing of a blog and includes a wide content, from choosing a blog name, to making a blog layout, changing the font on Blogger to adding social networking options to the blog.

How to Design Blogs

How to design blogs on popular blog platforms such as WordPress, Wix, and Tumblr.

Method 1. General Tips

1. Choose a blog topic: Before you even come up with a name or a color palette for your blog, you need to know what kind of content you'll use the blog to create. This is important for a couple of reasons:

- Direction: Knowing which direction your blog is headed will help inform your design choices (for example, an all-text blog might want to use expressive visuals to make it more appealing).

- Audience: You can get a general idea of who will be visiting your blog based on your topic, making it easier to determine how flamboyant or simple your blog should be.

2. Consider your ideal demographic: Based on your blog's topic, you should have an audience in mind, which will help you decide on a design theme later.

- For a blog about modern video games, for example, you might gear your content toward people in the 15 to 30 age range, meaning that you can experiment with different color schemes, visuals, and organization templates.

- If you're writing for an older, serious, research-driven audience, you'll most likely want to keep your blog fairly minimalist (e.g., black-and-white tones, simple font, minimal photos).

3. Name your blog: Naming your blog before you begin designing it will help inform some design decisions (such as your preferred title font), so come up with a title for your blog before you begin planning your blog's design.

4. Determine a consistent design: Whatever design philosophy you decide to use (e.g., minimalist), you'll need to employ it consistently throughout your blog.

- For example, every page of your blog should use the same design philosophy, not different ones.

- If you're still unsure of how you want to structure your blog's design, research current blog design trends. This will most likely provide the safest style of blog design.

5. Gather any resources that you'll need: These include pictures, videos, and content (e.g., text posts) that you want to post on your blog from the beginning.

- When actually designing your blog, it helps to have all of these resources in the same folder (e.g., the Desktop).

6. Decide on a blog platform: You'll find instructions for designing WordPress, Wix, and Tumblr blogs below.

- You'll want to remember your intended demographic while selecting a blog platform, as each platform has a slightly different tone and user base.

7. Begin designing your blog: A few common tips for doing so include the following:

- Use contrasting colors. Schemes such as black-and-white tend to appear cleaner than colors that clash (e.g., green and orange).

- Don't overcrowd the page. While visuals and sidebars are important, make sure that there's some white space (e.g., background) on the page. This will provide some relief for your audience.

- Use photos sparingly. Photos in particular can quickly crowd your page and take away from written content.

- Follow common Internet design conventions. These include things like having menu bars at the top of the page, search bars at the top of the page, additional links at the bottom of the page, and so on.

8. Update your blog's design as needed: You may find that your viewers have suggestions about certain aspects of the blog (for example, some may find that your link text is too hard to read); as such, you'll probably want to update your blog's design and layout to meet user needs.

Method 2. Using WordPress

1. Open WordPress' free site: Go to https://wordpress.com/ in your browser. WordPress is one of the most popular platforms for creating text-heavy blogs.

2. Enter your blog's basic information: This is the information that will be used to optimize your blog later. To do so:

- Click Get Started.

- Enter a title in the "What would you like to name your site?" text field.

- Enter a short description in the "What will your site be about?" text field.

- Select a goal by checking the box to the left of one of the options in the middle of the page.

- Select a comfort level.

- Click Continue

3. Create a URL for your blog: Type your preferred blog address name (e.g., the "facebook" part of "www.facebook.com") into the text box at the top of the page, then click the (name).wordpress.com entry, which should be at the top of the list of results.

- Unless you want to pay for a custom domain name, your blog will have to have ".wordpress.com" at the end of its address.

4. Scroll down and click Start with Free: It's a grey button at the bottom of the page. Doing so takes you to the account creation page.

5. Create your login credentials: These are the credentials which you'll use to log into WordPress later:

- Enter an email address in the "Your email address" text box.

- Enter a different username (if desired) in the "Choose a username" text box.

- Enter a password in the "Choose a password" text box.

- Click Continue.

6. Confirm your email address: You'll need to do this before you can begin customizing your Word-Press blog:

- Open the inbox for the email address that you used to create your login credentials.

- Select the "Activate (blog name)" email from WordPress.

- Click the blue Click here to Confirm Now button in the email's body.

7. Select a theme for your blog: Click Themes in the left-hand sidebar, then find a theme that you want to use, click it, and click Activate this design at the top of the theme's page. Your theme will serve as the base for your blog's design.

- Not all themes are free. You can filter the available themes into free-only by clicking the Free tab in the upper-right side of the Themes page.

8. Click Customize site when prompted. It's a blue button in the middle of the theme activation pop-up window. Doing so takes you to your blog's customization page.

9. Click the Site Identity tab. You'll find this on the left side of the page.

10. Edit your blog's basic presentation. While each theme will have slightly different options here, you can edit the following options for most blogs:

- Site Title: You can adjust the title that appears at the top of your blog here.

- Tagline: This text refers to the word, phrase, or description that goes below your blog's title.

- Any changes that you make will appear in the main WordPress window, allowing you to preview your changes as you go.

11. Return to the editing section: Scroll up and click < in the upper-left side of the page to do so.

12. Click Colors & Backgrounds: This option is on the left side of the page.

13. Edit your blog's color scheme and background: The Colors & Backgrounds section will vary depending on your selected theme, but you can usually select your preferred color palette for the blog, your preferred background image or color, and your preferred text color from here.

14. Return to the editing section: Scroll up and click the "Back" < button to do so.

15. Edit any other aspects of your WordPress blog: From this point, any other changes that you want to make will be made from within this menu.

- For example, if you want to add a new menu to your blog, you would click Menus, select the type of menu to add, and fill out any requested information.

- Keep in mind that the customization options for your blog will vary heavily depending on your selected theme.

16. Publish your changes: When you're satisfied with how your blog appears, click the blue Publish button at the top of the sidebar. This will save your blog's changes and publish it online for anyone to see.

Method 3. Using Wix

1. Open the Wix website: Go to https://www.wix.com/ in your browser. Wix allows you to customize virtually every aspect of your website simply by double-clicking an item or aspect that you want to change.

2. Create your Wix account: This is the account that you'll use to log into your Wix profile:

- Click Get Started in the middle of the page.

- Click the Sign Up link at the top of the page.

- Enter your email address and your preferred account password.

- Click Sign Up.

3. Click Blog: It's a link on the right side of the "What kind of website do you want to create?" page.

4. Click Choose a Template: This blue button is on the right side of the page. Doing so opens the Wix editor.

5. Select a template: Find a template that looks appealing to you, place your mouse cursor on it, and click the blue Edit button when it appears on the template's preview. This will open the template.

6. Click Start Now: It's a blue button near the bottom of the page.

7. Create a title: Double-click the placeholder title text, then type in the title that you want to use for your blog.

- You can edit the title's font, size, and color in the pop-up window that appears next to it when you double-click it.

8. Edit any other elements on the page: To edit an item, double-click it, then select new options for the item in the resulting pop-up menu.

- You can even change the background by double-clicking it and then selecting a background preset.

- The editing options will vary depending on the item that you want to edit and your selected template.

9. Publish your blog; When your blog matches your design expectations, click Publish in the upper-right corner of the page to save it.

- You can view your published site by clicking View Site in the resulting confirmation window.

Method 4. Using Tumblr

1. Open Tumblr's website: Go to https://www.tumblr.com/ in your browser. Tumblr is a relatively simple blog platform that doubles as a social media site, making it perfect for casual or image-heavy blogs.

2. Create your Tumblr account. This is how you'll log into your Tumblr blog later:

- Click Get Started.

- Enter an email address, username, and password.

- Click Sign up.

- Enter your age.

- Check the "I have read" box.

- Click Next.

- Check the "I'm not a robot" box.

3. Verify your email address. To do so:

- Open the inbox for the email address that you selected for your account.

- Open the "Verify your email address" email from Tumblr.

- Click the This is me! button in the email.

4. Select five topics to follow: Click at least five topics which you'd like to see in your dashboard. You'll have to do this before you can proceed.

5. Click Next: It's a blue button in the upper-right corner of the page. Your Tumblr dashboard will begin to load.

6. Open your blog's page: When the dashboard finishes loading, click the person-shaped Account icon in the upper-right side of the page, then click your blog's name in the drop-down menu.

- Your blog's name will be listed as your username toward the bottom of the page.

7. Click Edit appearance: It's an option in the upper-right side of your blog's page.

8. Scroll down and click Edit theme: This option is near the middle of the blog's settings page. Doing so opens the blog editor.

9. Select a theme for your blog: Click Browse themes near the top-left corner of the page, scroll down until you find a free theme that you like, click the theme to preview it, and click Use at the top of the sidebar to apply the theme to your blog.

10. Enter a title for your blog: Type your preferred blog name into the "Title" text field in the left-hand sidebar.

- This is the title that will appear at the top of your blog.

- You can also change your title's font, color, and size on most themes.

11. Edit any other theme options: Scroll through the sidebar and edit anything that you think should change on your blog. Your available design options will vary heavily depending on your selected theme, but you should have some of the following options for most blogs:

- Background Color/Image - This dictates the color and image that's used as your blog's background.

- Add a Page - If you scroll all the way down to the bottom of the sidebar, you will usually have this option, which allows you to add a page (e.g., a "Contact Me" page) to your blog. You can edit each page independently of your main page.

- Text Color or Body Color - This option determines the color of your text.

    - You'll often also see different color options for link text, title text, and so on.

12. Save your changes. When your blog's appearance is satisfactory to you, click the blue Save button at the top of the sidebar. This will save and publish your blog's changes.

How to Design a Blog Game

Have you ever wanted to play or make a blog game (non-virtual game made on blogs) but it got shut down or is inactive; maybe the people there aren't friendly to you? A blog game is a game (most commonly found on WordPress blogs) that you need to click on subpages, comment to buy stuff, and more! Here's how to make your own cool blog game. Written specifically for wordPress.

Steps

1. Decide whether you want to make it on your own current site or if you want to make the game have its own blog.

2. Once decided, go to the hosting blog and make a new page. Name it "Play", "Log On", "Start", or whatever you choose.

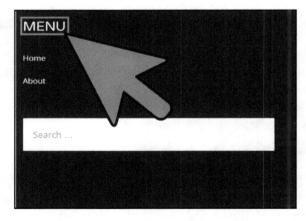

3. Create three main subpages: "Play", "Make an Account", and "Support". You can even add a developer's mini-blog, but many people prefer making the blog's "Home" page the developer's blog.

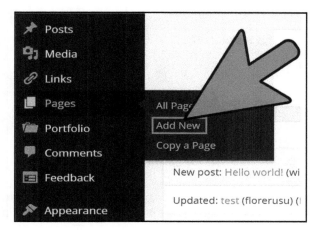

4. Keep making subpages (like "Town" could have "Bank" or a fashion store in it) with pictures of the content in it. People should be able to comment to buy stuff for their account.

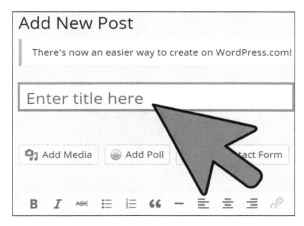

5. Do not include anything that people under age 18 through 0 months should not see, such as: Talk about drugs, talk about sexual stuff, etc.

6. Once you're finished, have one or two people beta-test it to see if it's any good or if the pictures are really showing up. They'll see the game from the player's point of view, not yours, the creator's point of view.

7. Copyright your work and decide whether you should have SOME of your content copyright-free or not, or if people interested in making their own versions of your content can get permission from you.

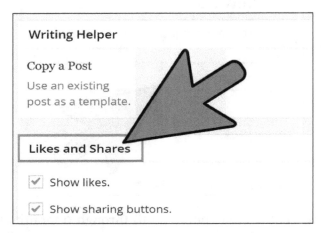

8. Once you're done, spread the word: Let everyone know it's there and have a grand opening "party" in the game, giving away a few items not available in the game's stores.

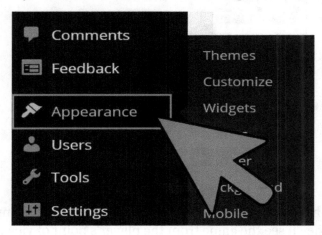

9. If it's virtual and automatic then it's better.

How to Give your Blog a Makeover

Viewers will not be likely to read your blog if it looks dull and unprofessional.

Steps

1. Look at other blogs: Do you see any you like? Make a list of all the things you like and dislike. Try to include some of the things you like from all the blogs in your blog.

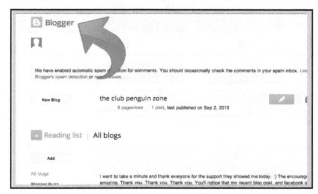

2. Come up with a writing plan: A "Coming Soon" feature with 3 upcoming big entries/articles will be useful to viewers and may entice them to visit your blog again.

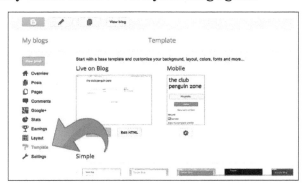

3. Play. Yes, play around with the tools, functions, gadgets, and extras. Which will be most useful to your blog type?

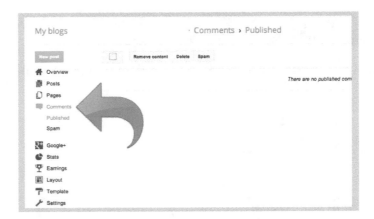

4. Accept and ask for feedback like comments. Blogger has a "Reactions" feature that you can customize to get quick and easy reader feedback so you can figure out what your writing style will be like.

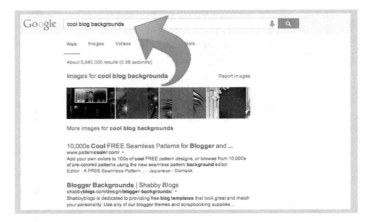

5. Get a cool background. A great website for free blog backgrounds is The Cutest Blog on the Block. This website has many, many backgrounds for your blog, plus instructions on how to add it in.

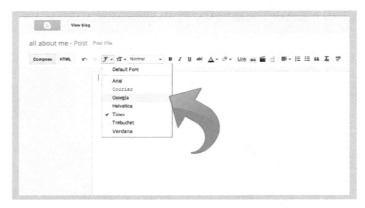

6. Experiment with font colors, sizes, and fonts. Make sure the words are not hard to read. Choosing a tiny font will not entice viewers to read your blog.

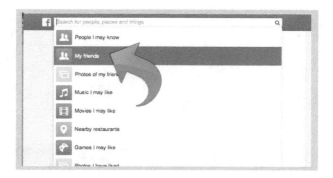

7. Tell people about your blog. Now that you have a blog makeover, get people to come see it.

How to Choose your Blog Name

One of the most important components of your blog's success is choosing the perfect name. The best blog names are unique, memorable, and relevant to the blog's content. To find the perfect name, brainstorm some ideas that capture the subject, tone, and vision of your blog, then refine them to appeal to your audience. Check to make sure the name is available across site domains and other social media networks, then make it official!

Part 1. Brainstorming Name Ideas

1. Incorporate your blog's niche: Your blog name should reflect what you'll be writing about, or your vision for the blog. Keep it general while you brainstorm, and consider your blog's most basic niche, then think of popular keywords related to that genre.

- Some of the most popular blog types include fashion, food, beauty, travel, photography, wedding, design, DIY, and fitness.

- If your vision for the blog is to promote health and fitness, choose some keywords related to that theme, such as "fit," "inspire," or "strong." If your blog is going to be all about photography, you could incorporate words like "lens," "focus," or "frame."

2. Make it unique: Think about what sets you and your blog apart. Incorporate a unique detail, such as where you live, your interests, your career, or a personal detail, like your hair or eye color. Using details like these in your can create a strong visual and make your blog more memorable.

- For example, ThePioneerWoman.com highlights the blogger's unique location and farm lifestyle, while BarefootBlonde.com references the blogger's iconic blonde hair.

3. Decide who your target audience will be: Knowing your target audience will help you choose a name that will perform well. Your target audience is the group of readers that you'll be writing for—think about their age, gender, income, career, and geographic location when you consider names.

- For example, if your target audience is made up of well-dressed, city-dwelling, college-educated women in their twenties, your blog name should appeal to an element of that lifestyle. For example, you could choose a name like "5th Street Fashion" or "Styleminded."

- Essentially, you want to avoid any misconceptions about your blog. Your name should make sense next to the content you post.

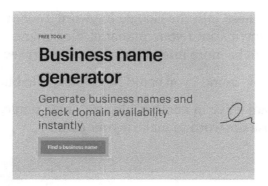

4. Use a name generator to get ideas: Using an automatic generator can take some of the pressure out of the process and get your imagination working. Use a site that lets you enter several keywords related to your blog, such as "health," "fashion," "food," or "photography." Even if you don't use these randomly generated names, you can still use them for ideas and inspiration.

- Some popular blog name generators include http://www.wordoid.com, which helps you create made-up words that are still understandable and unique, and http://www.namestation.com, which lets you plug in keywords and generates a list of possible names.

5. Look at competitors' blog names: Do some market research and check out blogs that are similar to yours. Consider what their names convey, how they sound, and how long they are. Draw inspiration from these names and apply their successful elements to your blog name.

6. Research related words and synonyms: Think of some of the keywords and topics you'll write

about on your blog and type these into the Google Keyword Tool or http://www.thesaurus.com. Try incorporating these synonyms into your potential blog names and see if any sound good. Sometimes a new synonym can be more interesting than an overused keyword.

- For example, instead of "home," you could try "abode," "habitat," "dwelling," or "hearth."

- If you like a certain adjective in another blogger's blog name, synonyms can help you re-imagine and repurpose the word to make it your own.

7. Explore your blog's tone: Think about how would you describe your voice and style of writing. Your blog name should reflect the tone, or the attitude that comes across in your writing, such as funny, nostalgic, warm, serious, or sarcastic.

- For example, if your writing is humorous and satirical, you'll want your blog name to reflect that tone. Readers will be able to recognize your style more easily if your blog name signals that tone right away.

Part 2. Refining the Name

1. Make sure your blog name is easy to pronounce: Multisyllabic or made-up words can be difficult

for a customer to pronounce, even when they're just reading in their head. Choose a name that won't confuse or trip up your readers. Use words that your target audience will recognize or a made-up word that's easy to understand, like "veganish" or "healthful."

- This will also help with memorability—a name that's easy to pronounce is much easier to remember.

2. Pick something short and easy to remember: Generally, you should limit your blog name to 1-3 words. Anything longer may be difficult to remember and can lose its catchiness. Long names also create awkwardly long domain names. Make sure your name is, at most, a catchy phrase rather than a full sentence.

- For example, you might shorten a name like "A London-Dweller's Travel Diaries and Memories" to "The London Diaries" or "London Lady Travels."

3. Don't use your own name in your blog name unless you plan on making it personal. If you use your name, you lose some authority as a general niche blog and end up pigeonholing your blog as more of a diary space. However, if you plan on making your blog all about your interests and your life, using your name may work.

4. Choose a name that will suit your blog for a long time: It's important to think about longevity when choosing your blog's name, so choose something that will still suit your content in years to come. However, if you do grow out of the name—for example, if your content changes or you find that readers have trouble remembering it—then choosing a new name and rebranding later on is a possibility.

- If you plan on making your blog extra-niche, choose a name that reflects that specialty and appeals to a very specific audience. For example, if you're a food blogger that only reviews pizza in New York City, you could use "The NYC Pizza Review" or "The NYC Slice."

- If you're worried about pigeonholing yourself and you'd like to leave room for content to evolve in the future, make your blog name something more general or abstract.

5. Consider how the name will look as a domain: When you write your blog name out as it will appear in someone's search bar (yourblogname.com), check for any issues that may arise. Your name may create some ambiguity if it can be read in multiple ways or inappropriately.

- For example, a humor blog called thereasonicantdance.com could be read as "The Reason I Can't Dance," "There a Son I Can't Dance," or "There a Sonic Ant Dance." Obviously, readers will realize the first option is the most likely, but if it gives them reason to pause, your name might need some work.

- Sometimes you need fresh eyes to spot a problem—have someone else read your domain name and tell you if they spot any confusing letter combinations.

Part 3. Confirming Availability

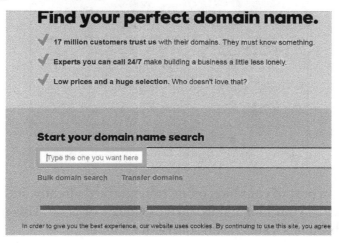

1. Check available site domains: If you're using a blogging service, such as Blogger or WordPress check your name's availability on their website. If you're building your own blog, check on domain purchasing sites to see if anyone else has a similar or identical name. If the name is taken, it's time to go back to the drawing board.

- Blogs with a ".com" URL are often much more popular and successful. Make sure to use an available .com domain name, rather than less popular options such as .net or .info.

- If you use blogging services, consider paying an extra fee to remove the ".blogspot" or ".wordpress" from your domain name. Having a simple ".com" domain looks much more professional and credible.

2. Check the availability of the name on social media: Once you've chosen a name, run it through various social media sites, such as Twitter, Facebook, and Instagram. If your handle is taken on too many sites, you should probably alter it a bit or choose a different name.

- You can also run the name through http://www.knowem.com, which will search all major social networks.

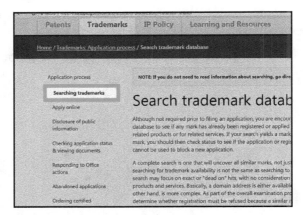

3. Make sure no one has a part of your blog name trademarked already. Be careful not to use trademarked company names in your blog name, such as Google or Nike. This may lead to legal issues, especially if your blog becomes a successful source of income.

How to Change the Font on Blogger

Tired of the boring old font on your blog, be Tired no more.

Steps

1. Log Into your blogger account using password/username.

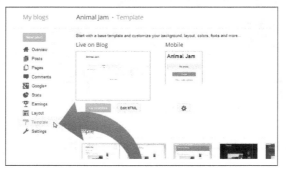

2. Click on the 'Template' link at the top right upper corner of your blog.

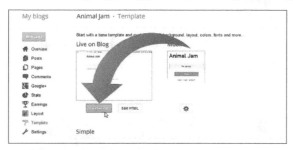

3. You will see an overview of your blog, and there will be button called 'Customize', click on it.

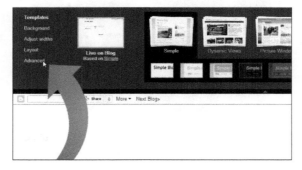

4. Enter in the whole layout of your blog and you can change what you want by clicking on the side column. To go and change the font, simply click on the 'Advanced' button in the side column.

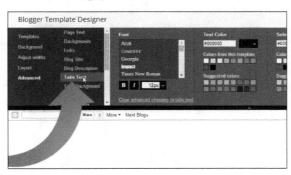

5. To change the font of your posts, simply click on 'Tabs Text.' Select your font, color and size.

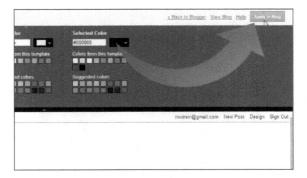

6. Now you're ready to go.

How to Make a Blog Layout

Design your blog layout for the best usability and search engine optimization at the same time. The best usable blogs do not exclude search engines.

Steps

1. Decide on left aligned versus centered: 68% of internet users have a screen resolution of either 1024x768, 1280x800, or 1280x1024, so obviously people are using larger monitors. You can take advantage of larger screen resolutions by using a center layout. Just design an adjustable layout so your blog is viewable on smaller screen resolutions. Visitors hate to scroll horizontally.

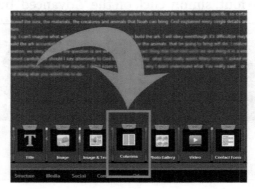

2. Pick the number of columns: Pick either a two column or three column layout. Make sure your content column isn't too wide. Thinner content columns make for easier reading.

3. Position your content: Tests show the best column for the blog post content is in the center. Visitors look for menu items and other action items in the left and right columns.

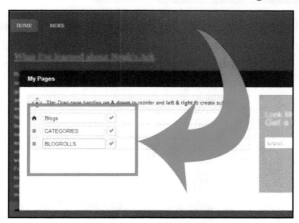

4. Outline your blocks: Examples: Social bookmarks, forms, blogrolls, categories, etc.

5. Split test different layout variables: Use a free split tester at Adwords.Google.com. Use the a/b tester if you are just starting your blog. It lets you test entirely different layouts and is meant for lower traffic blog pages.

6. Pick a color theme.

How to Add a Blog Background

Bloggers usually change blog backgrounds to make their blog more visually appealing for visitors. However, a background image that is added incorrectly can confuse the viewer and cause visitors to browse away from your blog. To add a blog background correctly it is important to use the correct HTML codes.

Steps

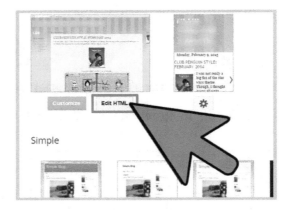

1. Go to the HTML page for your blog: If you are editing your blog offline then you can open it in Dreamweaver to change HTML. Blogging services like Blogger allow you to change HTML online by going to the Design page and selecting the "Edit HTML" tab. You need to be able to access the HTML codes for your blog, and how you do this can vary greatly depending on what blogging services and methods you use.

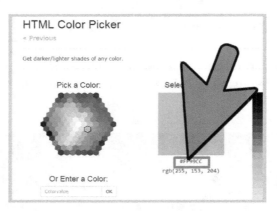

2. Don't try to look for a separate image with a different color if all you want to do is change the background color. Instead, you can just edit your HTML to change the existing color to the one that you want.

- Search for "HTML color chart" on the Internet. You should be able to find a table that displays different colors along with their color name and HEX (Hexadecimal) number. The HEX number is the number used within the HTML, so you need to remember the HEX number for the particular color that you want as your background.

- Find the code on your blog that defines the background color. It will look like this.

  ◦ body {

  ◦ background-color:#XXXXXX;

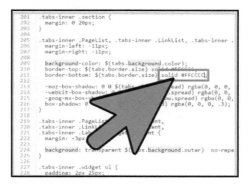

3. You will see the HEX number of the existing color instead of the X's displayed in the sample code.

- Change the HEX number to the number for the color that you want as your background. After you save and apply the new HTML, you will see the new color as the background.

Adding a Blog Background Image

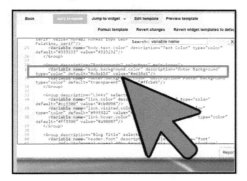

1. Select the image that you want to add as the background: There are many websites that allow you to download blog backgrounds or you can use an image that is already saved on your computer.

2. Upload the image: Photo hosting websites such as Picasa, Flickr and Photobucket allow you to

upload images for free. Your blog hosting service may also allow you to upload images in a similar way to how the rest of your blog is hosted.

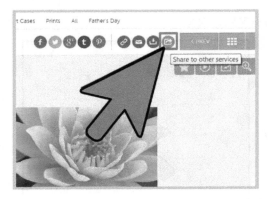

3. Get the image URL: To do this you need to open the image in your Internet browser and copy the URL where it is displayed.

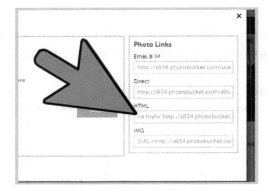

4. Insert the code for adding an image as the background. Here is the HTML code.

- body {

- background-image: url(image URL);

- You need to add the code where the body of your blog HTML begins. Replace "image URL" with the full URL where your image is located.

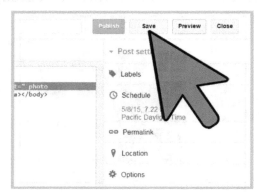

5. Save the changes after you edit HTML and view your blog. You should see the image added as the background.

How to Add a Counter to a Blog

A blog counter (also known as a hit counter) displays the number of times that your blog has been visited. You can add a counter to a blog not just as a visual element but also to count hits for measuring the blog's popularity. There are many websites that allow you to create counters and provide the HTML code that can then be used to add the counter to your blog.

Method 1. Free Easy Counters

1. Open the Free Easy Counters website.

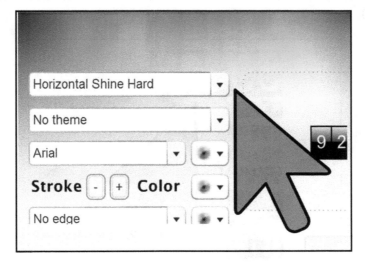

2. Put a dot next to the style of counter that you want to add to your blog.

3. Provide the URL of the page where you are going to add the counter.

4. Indicate what number you want the counting to start at (the default number is 0 but you can change it if you wish).

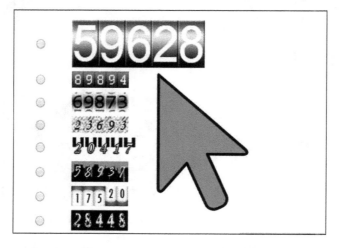

5. Select the number of digits that you want displayed by the counter.

6. Choose whether you want to count page views (how many times a page is viewed) or unique visitors (the number of different visitors who come to your website).

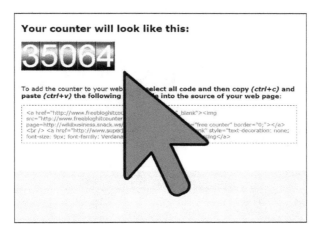

7. Notify Free Easy Counters if your website contains profanity by selecting "Yes." Otherwise you can select "No."

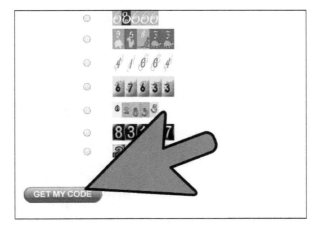

8. Press the button that says "Click Here To Get Your Counter Code Now." You will get the HTML code for the counter that you have created.

Method 2. Simple Hit Counter SHC

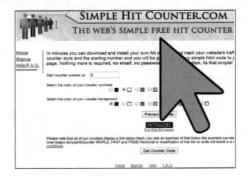

1. Go to the SHC website to start creating your counter.

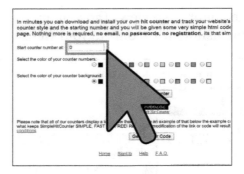

2. Type in the number you want to start counting from.

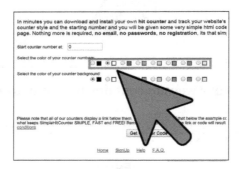

3. Mark a dot next to the color you want the numbers displayed in.

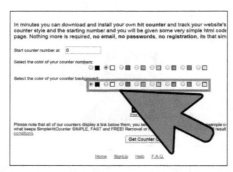

4. Pick the color that you want to use as the counter background.

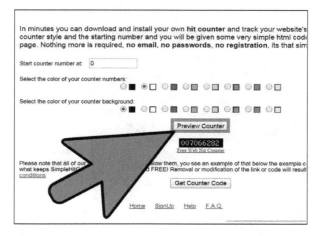

5. Hit the "Preview Counter" button to see what the counter will look like.

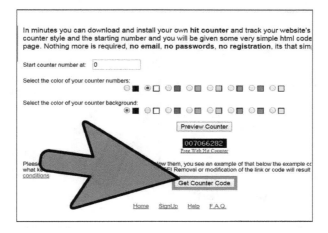

6. Click on the "Get Counter Code" to get the HTML code for the counter.

Method 3. Adding the Counter to Your Blog

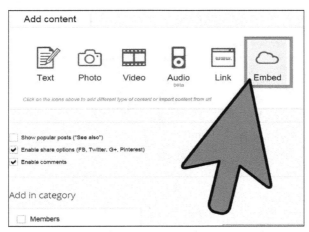

1. Open the HTML file for your blog homepage (you can use Dreamweaver or any other interface that allows you to edit the blog HTML).

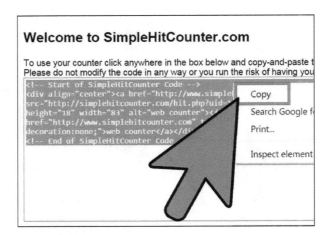

2. Copy the code that you had received from the website that you used to create your blog counter.

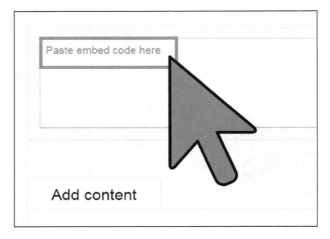

3. Paste the counter's HTML code in the area where you want it to be displayed within your blog's homepage HTML.

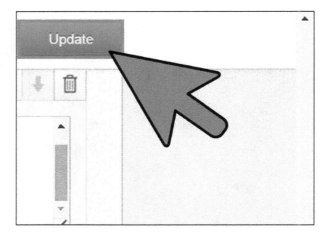

4. Save your changes and publish the new homepage online to replace the old one. You should see the counter added to your blog.

How to Add Bootstrap Navbar to Blogger

How to add bootstrap files and how to show bootstrap navbar in blogger is easier one. Using bootstrap will reduce the time to work in css codes of blogger and provides a clean design also reduce complexities in coding.It just need the time to place the code correctly in blogger.

Steps

1. First download bootstrap3.0 files from getbootsrap.com

2. Upload the bootstrap files to a hosting site like open drive or drop box. These files are bootstrap.min.css,bootstrap.min.js and get direct link or streaming link.

   • jQuery is necessary for Bootstrap's JavaScript plugins which helps for dropdown in navbar.

   • <script src='http://code.jquery.com/jquery-1.10.1.min.js'/><script src='http://code.jquery.com/jquery-migrate-1.2.1.min.js'/>

3. Go to your blogger account>>Template>>Edit html and below <head> add code which is in step5

- <meta content='width=device-width, initial-scale=1.0' name='viewport'/><link href='your direct link or streaming link url (min.css'media='screen' rel='stylesheet'/><script src='http://code.jquery.com/jquery-1.10.1.min.js'/><script src='http://code.jquery.com/jquery-migrate-1.2.1.min.js'/><script src='your direct link or streaming link url url(min.js) '/>

4. In between <body> ---- </body>, add code where you want.

- <nav class="navbar navbar-default" role="navigation">

  <button type="button" class="navbar-toggle" data-toggle="collapse" data-target=".navbar-ex1-collapse"> Toggle navigation</button> <a class="navbar-brand" href="#">Brand</a>

  - <a href="#">Link</a>

  - <a href="#">Link</a>

  - <a href="#" class="dropdown-toggle" data-toggle="dropdown">Dropdown </a>

    - <a href="#">Action</a>

    - <a href="#">Another action</a>

    - <a href="#">Something else here</a>

    - <a href="#">Separated link</a>

    - <a href="#">One more separated link</a>

  <form class="navbar-form navbar-left" role="search">

  <input type="text" class="form-control" placeholder="Search" />

  <button type="submit" class="btn btn-default">Submit</button> </form>

  - <a href="#">Link</a>

- ◦ <a href="#" class="dropdown-toggle" data-toggle="dropdown">Dropdown </a>

  - ◦ <a href="#">Action</a>

  - ◦ <a href="#">Another action</a>

  - ◦ <a href="#">Something else here</a>

  - ◦ <a href="#">Separated link</a>

</nav>

How to Add Social Networking Icons to your Blog

When you write a regular blog, you want to attract as many readers as possible to it. You also want your readers to share your blog with their friends, followers and connections. The best way to achieve these goals is to link your blog with your social networking sites. You can do this by adding social networking icons to your blog that will automatically link people to those sites with a simple click. Having easy to access and noticeable social networking icons on your blog will make it more successful. Add social networking icons to your blog by locating the images you want, uploading them to your blog and including a brief HTML code that will customize the icons to your site.

Steps

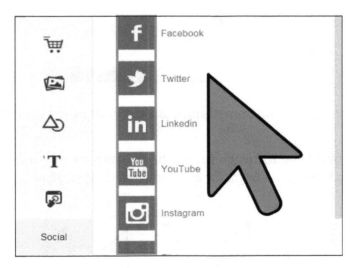

1. Decide which social networks you want to list on your blog. The most popular icons include Facebook, Twitter, LinkedIn and Pinterest.

- Choose social networking spots where you and your blog readers are active. For example, if you have a great Facebook page, you will want to include that icon. If you want to encourage your readers to pin your blog onto their Pinterest boards, be sure you have that icon present.

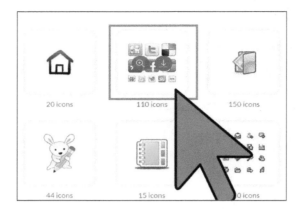

2. Locate the best icons for your blog: You can download standard icons for all of the social networking sites at several websites, including IconArchive, Web Designer Depot and Icon Dock. An Internet search of "social icons" will provide several other options.

- Use updated and easily recognizable icons. It is okay to be creative, but make sure your readers can recognize the link provided by your icons. For example, most Twitter icons are a small "t" with a light blue background or an image of the Twitter bird. If you change the color, you might confuse people.

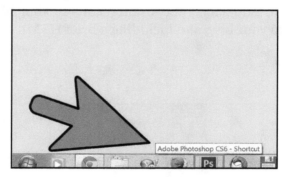

3. Create your own icons if you want something different. You might want the icons to match the design of your blog.

- Use Photoshop or Adobe InDesign for the best results in creating your own icons. Try to keep your design to 60px by 60px for easy downloading and linking.

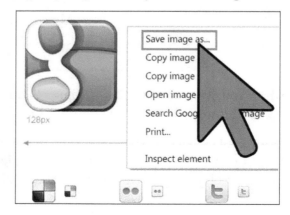

4. Download the icon images you plan to use onto your computer. This is as easy as saving it in a file on your machine.

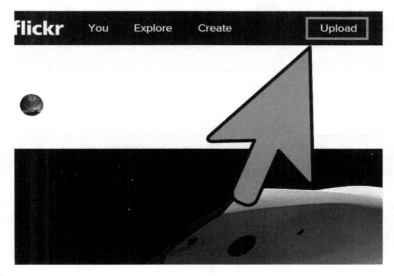

5. Upload your icon images to a photo site such as Flickr or Photobucket if you often use these sites to place pictures and graphics on your blog.

- Add the images to your media library in WordPress if that is the blogging platform you use.

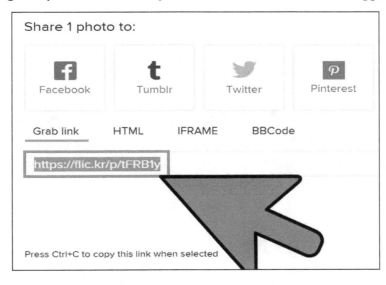

6. Check to make sure each image you have uploaded has a URL (this stands for uniform resource locator).

- Look for the URL in WordPress by clicking on the image in your library. You will notice the URL in the "File URL" field. It will start with the letters "(http." http.")

- Find the URL on photo sharing sites by clicking "share" when you let your mouse hover over the image. You will see a "get link code" tab, and the link will be displayed. The letters "(http" http") will be the start of the URL.

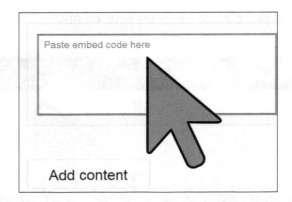

7. Find the right spot for the HTML code, which will depend on the blogging platform you use. Most blogs are created on WordPress or Blogger.

- Place the code in the HTML widget area on Blogger. For WordPress blogs, place the code in the text widget area.

8. Add the following HTML code: "http://www.linkgoeshere.com" target="_blank"><img src="http://www.imageurlhere.com".

- Put a link to your own social networking page where it says "link goes here" and put the image's URL where it says "imageurlhere."

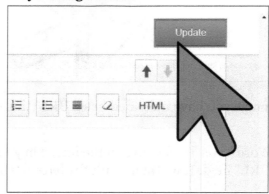

9. Run a test: Have a friend pull up your blog and click on the social networking icons you have included. Make sure it takes the user to the right place.

Permissions

Index